FREE-FALLING

True Stories of One Man's Leap into the Miraculous

by Chuck Parry

Free-Falling

True Stories of One Man's Leap into the Miraculous

Copyright ©2010 by Chuck Parry
All rights reserved

Unless otherwise noted, all Scripture quotations are from the Holy Bible,
New King James Version. Copyright © 1979, 1980, 1982 by Thomas Nelson, Inc.
Used by permission. All rights reserved.

ISBN-10: 1453748784

ISBN-13: 978-1453748787

cparrybusiness@gmail.com

Additional copies may be ordered directly from this address:

https://www.createspace.com/3475080

Printed in the United States of America

DEDICATION

I dedicate this, my first real adventure in book writing, to my family who shared the journey and lived through many of these escapades with me: my wife Linda and our three children, Faith, Grace, and Jesse. This is the real heritage I leave to you, and to my grandchildren, Christopher and Chiara. May you be blessed with many years of life-transforming adventures and miraculous encounters of your own, always finding love and abounding with fun!

ENDORSEMENTS

Chuck is like one of those storytellers of old, but his stories are not fables or fairy tales; they are Holy Spirit adventures. I am honored and challenged when I hear his stories, and also grateful to participate in new adventures with him!

— *Geir Christian Johannssen, Krakstaad, Norway*

Chuck is a Legend. After hearing the stories of his life and journey, I am constantly finding myself responding with the phrase: "You've gotta be kidding me, Chuck!" Just when you think you have heard it all, he busts out another one of his everyday stories from the massive archive, and your mind is blown away again. The thing I love about hearing these stories is that they're not just a few moments in his life, but for Chuck they have proven to be characteristic of his lifestyle — to expect the impossible, to believe for the miraculous in a childlike way, and to step out in faith and be a part of what God is currently doing today. What an adventure to walk with our God the way He intended us to. People who think following God is boring must hear a bit of Chuck's life and they'll reconsider.

— *Gabriel Adam Pepperd, Wasilla, Alaska*

This book is not just a personal recollection of historical events; it is an invitation to experience the same supernatural adventures as Chuck and to come to know the source behind his supernatural friendship. Chuck Parry retells his story in a way that almost enables the reader to see, taste, smell, and touch what Chuck has experienced. What impresses me the most is that Chuck continues to live this adventure in the supernatural day by day. This is real!

— Andy Mason, Hastings, New Zealand

ACKNOWLEDGEMENTS

Sally Valin ~ this book would not look or read like it does today without your tireless efforts at editing and your attention to detail. Your standard of excellence makes me look great. I'm grateful to have you for a sister and friend.

Brad Webster ~ your creative abilities have gone further than cover design. Thanks for your coaching in every area.

Aaron McMahon ~ your affirmation, encouragement, and empowerment inspired me to believe the seemingly impossible: I can write this book!

Andy Mason ~ thanks for being my first writing partner and an awesome coach and friend.

My International Transformation Writers Group ~ you all kept me going and made me feel like "the World's Greatest Writer"! I miss gathering and listening to one another read our latest works. You are all amazing!

My supportive wife Linda ~ thank you for giving me the time to write and for believing in me. You are beloved, brave, and beautiful!

All of my friends all over the planet ~ thanks for continually affirming and encouraging me to write. Your continual expectation of the finished work makes me feel clothed in greatness. I love you all; you're part of the adventure.

FOREWORD

In 1983 I met Chuck and Linda Parry. We had just started going to a little Assembly of God church in a small town in Western Colorado. Chuck and I both had an interest in youth and started taking groups of teenage boys on three-day backpacking trips. I do not remember one trip without some kind of miracle taking place. Prior to one of the earlier trips into the San Juan Mountains we'd seen clouds and rain engulfing the high country every day for over two weeks. We'd planned the trip already, so off we went. Sure enough, by one o'clock in the afternoon it was raining, I mean really pouring; everything was soaking wet. We kept hiking and praying, and Chuck was believing for something special. Just as evening approached we came upon a cabin all dried in, with dry firewood to boot. This was a blessing, as it continued to rain all through the night.

The next day we'd planned to hike Uncompahgre Peak, a fourteener, and for the first time in weeks we awoke to clear, blue skies! It was beautiful; not a cloud appeared all day! The boys recognized it as unusual, and we all kept declaring, "God has given us this day." When we reached the top of the peak we started to pray and express thanks to God for His blessing, and as we said "Amen" we looked up and an eagle swooped right by us, and he was so close it seemed we could have touched him. We followed him as he disappeared over the north rim, and as we raced to the edge we found ourselves looking down the face of a sheer cliff. Partway down was an eagle's nest where he was feeding three eaglets!

*"Those who wait on the Lord shall renew their strength,
they shall mount up with wings as eagles..."*

That began a 28-year relationship that continues to this day. Since then we have worked, played, laughed, cried, and ministered together in all kinds of places. Chuck has an incredible and simple gift of faith. He reads God's word and simply believes it. Because of this I've seen so many things come so easily for him, which is sometimes aggravating. I have seen myself and others struggle with truths of the bible, yet he has this simple way of reading it, believing it, and then he starts to live it out. Working with him at the Rainbow Gatherings has been the most rewarding experience of my life. Starting off in the early years with just seven or eight people doing all the work, we've watched it grow into hundreds coming to help. Through the years it has been the one event that has most significantly changed and encouraged my walk with God. We have seen many people changed, introduced to God, healed, delivered, food multiplied, and all sorts of signs and wonders. We have all heard the old saying, "You can lead a horse to water, but you can't make him drink." Chuck has this way, I guess it's like leaking salt, that makes you want to drink more and more. What he leaks is contagious. Being around him always makes me thirsty for more. I love his love for the Holy Spirit; he's always wanting to hear and obey. I love his love for people, always wanting them to be built up in their gifts and become all they can become in God. I love his love for joy. That may seem weird, but I've noticed that when we see someone crying in a moving meeting, we say: "Oh, God is moving on him;" yet when someone starts to laugh in a meeting we often get offended. Chuck has the ability to release joy. Real joy that comes from the fact that we are loved outrageously by an Almighty God. Joy that looks difficulties in the face and laughs.

"Rejoice always, pray without ceasing,
in everything give thanks."

Chuck demonstrates this as a military stance and always comes out victorious. I hope this book will challenge all who read it to believe for more; to go out to the edge and jump, for God is faithful in all that He has promised.

— *Jody Segura, Cedaredge, Colorado*

CONTENTS

INTRODUCTION 1

Chapter 1 **ANYTHING IS POSSIBLE** 3
A Tent in the Storm; Introduction to God; A Cabin in the Mountains; God Gives Me the Farm

Chapter 2 **RAISED FROM THE DEAD** 17
Bike Ride to Heaven; Reading the Book; The Baptism in the Holy Spirit; Miracle in a Blizzard; Shifting the Atmosphere; 320 Miles to the Gallon; Grace is Healed; Another Blizzard Miracle; Let's Get High and Read the Bible

Chapter 3 **100% COMMITMENT** 43
That Boy is Dead; Full Moon on Hart's Basin; Breakdown ~ Shift Happens; Hordes of Grasshoppers; Arthritis Healed; Cancer Healed; Knocking on Doors; The Amazing Deliverance of a Navajo Man; I Can't Hear You, God; Brain Tumor Healed; Backpacking Through the Grand Canyon; The Shirt Shrinks; Building a Camp by Faith; The Village Idiot

Chapter 4 **RAISING THE DEAD** 75
Grandma Comes Back from Death; Spying Out the Land; County Jail; Crack-House Drunk; Rebuking Death in Uganda; Baby Comes Back to Life Over Skype

Chapter 5 **REVIVAL IN RUSSIA** 99
Always Triumphant; Divine Connections; Moscow University; Supernatural Evangelism; Great Favor; He is Jealous for Me; Victor and Victor

CONTENTS

Chapter 6 **THE BREAD OF LIFE KITCHEN** 129
The Rainbow Gathering; Becoming a Kitchen in
Colorado; Transformations in Wyoming; Bumming a
Cigarette; All-Night Drums in Our Kitchen; Gutter
Punks; Authority Over Flies and Mosquitoes; Water
From Heaven; Food-Line Healing; Drum-Circle
Deliverance; Pure Love

Chapter 7 **MULTIPLICATION OF FOOD** 161
Elk-Steak Fajitas for 400 ~ Again; Multiplication of
Money; Abundance Always; Morning Meetings;
Fourth of July Rainbow Style; Raising the Dead in
Wyoming; Main Meadow Healing Revival

Chapter 8 **AUTHORITY OVER THE WEATHER** 191
Arizona National Rainbow Gathering; Commanding
the Storm in California; Climbing Mount Sneffels;
Outdoor Weddings; Glory ~ Many Nations, One
Voice

Chapter 9 **SOME ADVENTURES INTO THE
UNSEEN REALMS** 215
Thin Places; The Throne Room; The King on a
Horse; Transported?; "... Unusual Miracles ..."

Chapter 10 **BROKERING HEAVEN** 225
The Prophecies; The Encounter; The Hot Tub

AFTERWORD 233

xiii

INTRODUCTION

Adventures are experiences we love to remember, to talk about and retell to stir the hearts, or to illustrate a point, or simply to top the other guy's tale. Sometimes we like to plan them, dreaming of where we'd go or what we'd do. But the true adventures we never plan. They have a way of reaching out and taking us, of capturing us. And when you find yourself feeling like you're standing in the open door of a plane at 10,000 feet, and the pit of your stomach is somewhere in your throat, and you're looking out into open space with nothing more tangible before you than *air,* and it's time to *leap* out into it, and you *think* you have a parachute in the pack on your back and you're *almost* certain it will open, then you can be sure *the adventure is about to begin.*

That's how I always feel when I leap into the miraculous. The unseen realm is just too *invisible* and we can't grab hold of it very securely. But I'm certain it's what we're created for. That's why we've got to get to know the One who *made* it. Because *He* holds *us* very securely. And regardless of the conundrum or the impossibility, He's never dropped me once. That's what these stories are about.

And that's what led me to write this book. It all started with the stories. When our children were young, we'd take them camping and we'd lie in our sleeping bags under the open sky filled with a billion stars, and I'd tell them stories of miracles that had happened in their lives. Then when I taught high school Shop class in the early

1

'80s, those bad boys would ask me to tell them some stories, and they loved listening to them. They said they'd never heard such stories. Later, when my wife Linda and I started a community of spiritual adventurers in a small mountain village, the stories were retold. And when the amazing people who were being drawn to that little community from five surrounding counties began to become radically alive, then new stories were birthed. Each one seemed to contain and impart the inspiration to be duplicated and surpassed. Later, when I was asked to speak at gatherings of remarkable and fun and diversely unique individuals in places like Georgia and Idaho, those people began to ask me to write the stories down. I still remember the situations, the faces, the sincerity, and the stirring in my heart each time someone would tell me that I needed to write a book of the stories. I've been thinking about it for years.

Chapter One

ANYTHING IS POSSIBLE

A TENT IN THE STORM

We were driving up the coast of Northern California in the spring of 1980. Mount Saint Helens had just erupted and we were heading north toward Oregon and right into it. Pretty exciting. As night fell, the little VW station wagon was low on gas so we pulled into a small coastal town. This was before credit-card pumps, and way before credit cards for us. The only gas station we'd seen for miles was closed, and so was every other building in sight. As we continued on toward the next town, I realized we would not make it on the gas we had. We'd have to camp for the night and return in the morning to fill up.

I pulled over onto a treeless grassy meadow at the top of a rocky cliff high above the ocean. The surf was pounding below and a strong sea breeze blew over us. Linda and I made a bed on the grass with blankets and sleeping bags for our two daughters and ourselves — Faith was three and Grace was about six months old. The

3

stars overhead were just beginning to disappear behind huge black clouds rolling in from the ocean. Wind, lightning, and thunder started to increase, and it was obvious that a big storm was brewing. All eyes were turned on me. I stood on that grassy embankment and I looked into the unseen realm and I saw it.

"I'm going to make a huge bubble over us and it will keep us dry all night just like a tent."

That seemed to satisfy everyone, so I stretched out my arms overhead and declared it, and then we all hopped into bed to the sound of rain falling. In the morning we awoke to find the grass all around us was soaking wet, but the circle that contained our bed was completely dry.

Things like that have been happening ever since I first met this amazing God.

INTRODUCTION TO GOD

It all started with the bridge experience when I was a college student in 1972. It was springtime, and all the winter ugliness of the big city was being replaced with exhilarating new life. Ten of us, high on LSD, were heading across Philadelphia on foot after an outdoor rock concert just as the sun was beginning to set. Suddenly we approached a six-lane major thoroughfare teeming with rush-hour traffic — a definite obstacle to reaching our destination. Stumbling into each other, some of us headed north for Walnut Street, while others tried to go south. I looked ahead and spotted it: *a bridge!* Well, sort of. It was a set of four steel I-beam bridge trusses silhouetted against the sunset — a bridge under construction. Long black, curving arches spanned the traffic, each about eight inches wide along the top edge.

"Come on, a short cut!"

I headed out first, like a tight-rope walker, out and up onto the middle of the arch above the rushing traffic.

"It's easy, see?"

Ve-erry tentatively one crept out, then another. I led them by the hand, one by one, over to the other side — three, four, five of them. The drama was intense.

And then came that moment, frozen in time, as I stood in the middle of the "bridge" and looked down. Instant death and destruction sped by in six lanes, 30 feet below. I looked ahead: some of the group were safely on the other side and a few were nearly there, creeping cautiously along. Looking back, I saw one on his hands and knees, crawling. One girl was on her belly with her arms and legs wrapped around the steel girder, looking down, eyes wide, wailing. There I was, leading them to the other side. I stood in the Philadelphia sunset, and the noise of the traffic faded out and everything became completely still. And then it came — not from outside, yet clearly not my own thoughts. A voice clear and calm and sure:

"You could be doing this for Me."

And there it all was: the narrow bridge over death and destruction, the safety of the other side, the sudden gravity and responsibility of the situation — life and death. And I looked up into the sky, tilted my head to one side, and in total wonderment said:

"HUH?"

With a shake of my head I went back to the job of getting everyone across. And then off we went ... our own way.

But things were never quite the same after that. All my answers to life and my psychedelic view of the spiritual realm didn't satisfy me. For a while I seemed to get it more together; I even went to classes and did some homework. Somewhere there was a purpose for me. I didn't know it then, but I felt a pull that made me want to respond; a stirring that caused me to start searching.

A CABIN IN THE MOUNTAINS

I graduated from the university that year, a miracle in itself, and went back to New England, to a farm in New Hampshire, looking for answers and a purpose in a simpler life. That summer I became involved in the largest drug deal of my life. It entailed driving a BMW sports car from New Hampshire to San Francisco and trading it to purchase a huge quantity of LSD, which I brought back on a commercial airliner in a backpack.

I'd stopped in Colorado en route and climbed around in the mountains, exploring the vastness of the Rockies. There I encountered monumental strength and rugged beauty in an outrageous display of creativity and variety. I was inspired and immensely stimulated. It took my breath away. It left me speechless, yet at the same time I felt the blood pumping in my veins. I stood on a mountaintop and looked at my *hands*, and it was as if I were seeing them for the first time. I was incredibly *alive*. Right there the thrill of the drug adventure left me, and I went on to complete the trip with an overwhelming desire to return to the mountains and seek ... what? Peace of mind? Cosmic consciousness? The Creator of it all? Is it God; is God real? Could I encounter God? Could I have a real experience with God? Is God more than a concept, more than a consciousness, more than a "Force"? Could I find God in the midst of this vast cosmos? Is God personal, relational? If so, could I meet Him, experience Him, know Him? I was really curious.

In California I was in two automobile accidents on two consecutive days. Each time someone plowed into my rear end while I was stopped at an intersection; each time I was driving a different vehicle. The first time it was the BMW. The second time I was driving a friend's rusted-out old junker of a Chevy convertible that was full of dirty clothes and, literally, held together by coat hangers. As I was trying to find the fork that had fallen off the dashboard on impact (and which I needed to pry open the glove box to get to the registration), the guy who had hit me was pulling out cash to pay me off so I wouldn't report the accident. He was an insurance salesman and this was his fifth accident that summer. I was left with the over-whelming feeling of having been kicked in the butt by someone to get me to leave that life and move on to something else ... but what? Truly I was tired of the drug life: false identities and paranoia, people carrying guns, a friend paralyzed by a bullet in the spine, young men setting themselves up as drug lords and gods.

There was a great desire growing in me to change everything about my life, without having the slightest idea how to pull it off. A new location sounded good, and the mountains sounded great. It's amazing how much resistance we can experience when we try to change the

7

course of our journey while we're racing along at full speed. It seemed like I was cranking the wheel for a directional change without much help or encouragement from other people, from "the Force" or any other spiritual entity, or even from God, if God was there.

Back in New Hampshire, I settled my affairs and told my friends I was heading out to Colorado. And suddenly the obstacles and the hurdles appeared. First some friends thought it was a great idea — "Chuck's off on an adventure; let's go along." The same relationships and lifestyle I was trying to flee wanted to come along, to follow me. And then I began to encounter a lot of religious fanatics with their talk about consciousness and gurus. I ended up in a large cabin in the mountains with sometimes 20 people dropping in from Denver as well as from the east and west coasts.

I turned sour and growled and withdrew. I remember one day sitting on the roof of the house, just after Christmas, watching people as they drove in from skiing and out to other places. They had to come up on the roof to talk to me. Gradually all the people dispersed. I can still see the face of the girl I'd been living with as she turned to look out of the rear window of the Volkswagen; she gave me a cautious smile and a wave as the car disappeared down the road.

And I felt free that day. And the snow came and my car broke down and I ran out of food and it kept snowing and I went inside to wait it out ... and I crossed a threshold of anticipation and expectancy.

And at last I was *ALONE*.

Except, there was this guy who was into some Indian

guru he'd discovered when he was in prison on a drug bust. He was helping me put my car back together in a garage down the mountain and he kept feeding me a mixture of Hindu-American thought and cosmic consciousness. Everything I was experiencing seemed to be a peripheral distraction from the strange pull I was feeling in my heart. But I needed more than a Force. I needed a real and relational God! I knew, somehow really knew deep inside, that if God were real I should be able to experience Him; He would want me. He was somehow reaching out to me.

There was nothing left — the money, friends, pride, social standing, education, thrills ... they were all gone. It was just me and the oatmeal in this cabin in the snow. For a week I lived on oatmeal, every meal. No butter, milk, brown sugar. Just oatmeal. And I loved it. Everything was getting simpler, like oatmeal. Then one night a week later, after working on my car down the mountain, I stopped in at my mechanic friend's kitchen door and, while talking, spied a cube of butter on his counter.

"Butter!"

"Yeah. Hey, you want it?"

"Really? Could I?"

"Hey, take it, man, it's yours."

Off I went into the night, boots squeaking on the snow. The crystal black sky was pulsing with stars, and there was the old toenail moon and my frozen breath as I huffed up the mountain with my treasure in the pouch of my overalls, close to my heart. Home to a bowl of oatmeal, with *butter*.

I didn't know how to pray in those days; but I would talk to God. *"I want to know You. How can I know You, God?"*

I had one book, the "Tao Te Ching" by Lao Tsu. It spoke of the virtuous man and what he would do, the choices he would make. I was definitely *not* the virtuous man. How do I become the virtuous man? Do I want to? Wisdom and excellence were alluring, but I wasn't sure I knew *how* to make excellent or virtuous choices.

And I had some Grateful Dead records. (*Vinyl records* – this was 1972.) Nothing was happening and God seemed unattainable, and I was discouraged and ready to quit. Right then this Jerry Garcia song came on:

*"Won't you try just a little bit harder,
Couldn't you try just a little bit more ..."*

And I'd concede and try again: *"God, I want to know You, experience You, encounter You. How can I know You?"*

And the answer came in the morning.

The sun rose brilliantly in the clear sky, a blinding light reflected on the snow outside the windows of the dark cabin. I prayed. Suddenly the room was full of light, brighter than outside, and I was overwhelmed by the presence of *Jesus*. I didn't see Him and He didn't talk, but I knew it was He. I hadn't been looking for *Him*. I hadn't made that connection and had not expected to encounter Jesus. Why *Him*? And suddenly something in me knew why, and I heard a saying in my head:

*"I am the Way, the Truth, and the Life.
No one comes to the Father except through Me."*

10

And then I did something that was an honest cry from my real place of need — I asked Him to be my Guru, my Teacher. I knew that I needed one, and I felt so emptied of my own self-importance that I was really, finally ready to learn. I actually knelt down in the Presence of something supernatural and awesome and surrendered myself to Him.

I left that cabin a changed man, or maybe even a man for the first time. There were values and habits that changed so fast I didn't know what was happening. No more drug dealing. I got a job. I cared about other people. I started listening, looking, searching ... but for what? And then Wisdom, Excellence, and Virtue began to ambush me.

I stayed in the mountains and lived out of a backpack, even in the snow, because there I felt safe with God. Even while I was working construction, I'd drive into the mountains at the end of the day, put my pack on, and hike up to a good camping spot, sometimes in the dark. I'd get out my stove and cook a meal and talk to God, and then watch the stars appear and wonder at the vastness of the universe. I'd ask questions, and then somehow I'd know the answer, and right when the answer would come to me a huge shooting star would zip across the sky like an exclamation point! God didn't speak much, but the conversations were powerful and stimulating. By the summer I was working in the fruit orchards of Western Colorado and saving money for a tipi. I loved the mountains, and a tipi was really glorified camping, with a fire inside and all ... but I dreamed of growing my own food. So I talked to God about it.

GOD GIVES ME THE FARM

It was in the early spring of 1974 that I began asking God about farming. Then I met Larry. He was a doctor from Chicago who had taken LSD and gotten into a purple school bus with his wife and three kids and taken to the road. They ended up in Western Colorado and bought a farm, and it became a hippie commune. So Larry invited me to move my tipi down to his place on Redlands Mesa and join them. I thought I'd check it out.

The spring weather was still cold and the trees were bare, but the earth smelled dank and rich. I was hitchhiking down valley when an old farmer and a young woman picked me up. They were heading to Delta, the county seat about 30 miles west, and asked where I wanted to go. Well, I knew the farm was up on Redlands Mesa, but I didn't know where, so I told them that if they could head me in that direction I knew the Lord would get me there. The old gentleman's eyes brightened and he got a little excited as long as we were bringing the Lord into it. The woman knew the neighbors of the farm I was seeking and felt sure that if we got close she'd recognize the place. So we took off on an adventure up country roads, past orchards and ranches, conferring at every crossroad until we came to a consensus, and amazingly we never took a wrong turn. Within about 45 minutes we stopped in front of a somewhat dilapidated farmhouse surrounded by still-leafless cottonwoods. We looked at each other and agreed that this was definitely the place. There was some hugging and the old man blessed me, and it felt like we were old friends as I stepped out of the truck in front of the driveway. It was the strangest thing: though I had never seen the place, I felt as if I were coming home as I walked up the drive.

I moved my tipi there the next week, setting it up on a grassy bank by the creek, with acres of sagebrush behind me and a view of the fields to the east. I could see mountains in the distance for 360 degrees around me; there were very few trees, and the sky was vast and open overhead. I was on the far side of the 80 acres, while the rest of the folks lived in the farmhouse, barn, and school buses clustered up at the road. It didn't take me long to wonder what I was doing there, as the relationships were strange on the farm. Individually the people were interesting and unique, but their interactions were dramatic and confusing. One morning I decided to stay at my tipi, and spent the day just messing around and talking to God.

"Is this where I'm supposed to be? This is the most confusing place I've ever been. Are You sure, God?"

But He kept reassuring me that He had it under control.

"Trust Me."

When I walked across the fields later that evening I found the whole place deserted, and Larry came by and told me there'd been a big fight, the sheriff had gotten involved, everybody was moving away, and he was leaving and going back to being a doctor. Did I want to stay and farm the place? It felt like God was laughing.

I lived on the farm for 15 years and built a house there. Friends joined me that first year and we combined the farm with their 40 acres across the road. We built a root cellar, barns, and a chicken house and cultivated a two-acre truck garden in addition to farming 80 acres of field crops. Though people came and went over the years, we worked as a cooperative, each creating our own housing and each taking on some aspect of the work, and we all shared in the harvest. For the first few years we ate only what we raised; we raised our own beef, lambs, turkeys, chickens for meat as well as layers, goats for milk, bees for honey, wheat, blue corn, potatoes, beans, and a variety of other things. We canned and froze all our fruits and vegetables to get us through the winter. It was a healthy, satisfying, hard-working life, and later that summer a beautiful blonde-haired girl came from Oregon and pitched her tipi across the creek from mine. Three years later Linda and I were married right there on the farm.

We had both been searching to know God and had both dreamed for years of farming. Though we had tried out a wide variety of spiritual pursuits, He had been radical in His relentless and faithful pursuit of us. It was there on the farm that we really began to fall in love with Him.

One day in 2009 while I was writing this book, He opened up His Father-God-home-videos-of-the-kids collection from this era and gave me a glimpse that filled my heart to overflowing with how much He loved me. I saw this 25-year-old boy, barefoot and tanned brown by the summer sun, wearing just some old gym shorts, galloping through acres of sagebrush at full speed, hurdling the bushes as he zig-zags across the mesa top wearing a huge smile from ear to ear. He leaps the creek and slows to a fast walk in the soft tall grass of the creek bank, where he follows the trail his own bare feet have made, skimming the seed tops of the myriad varieties of grasses with his fingertips as he takes a leap, spins around, and scares up a cluster of little yellow butterflies which spiral up around him as he looks up into the sky and shouts: "God, I love You!" For a moment he stands still, feet spread apart feeling the cool moist earth under the trampled grass, and his hands reach up in the air as he sees a night hawk circle above — it makes a dive right over him and makes that ripping sound in its swift descent, then pulls up at the last moment and sweeps away. *Thank You,* the boy whispers in his heart. And I'm watching the movie in my head and I'm inside the boy again, and I remember how sweet it is to first fall in love.

I used to love drawing and painting, but when I started farming God gave me a different canvas. He showed me the young man on the old Massey 65 tractor discing a field in the springtime that had been plowed in the fall. I remembered how I loved to crisscross the field with furrows and then make sweeping curves and circles until I had something like a Japanese raked-sand garden, but this one covered six acres and the only One who could see it all was God. I'd look up and ask Him how He liked it.

Another time I climbed to the top of a nearby mountain and looked out at the vastness of the Colorado Rockies — 14,000-foot peaks in waves spreading into the distance. I felt so insignificant that I asked:

"God, do You really know me? Am I only a speck in this great expanse?"

Just then I looked across at a mountain miles away and saw a dark speck in the air above it. The speck began to move toward me and made huge circles as it soared in the sky. It spiraled closer and closer and grew larger and larger as it headed across the valley toward me. I watched as the bald eagle flew my way in giant sweeping curves until it came to a stop directly above me, huge and impressive, hovering on an updraft. It stayed there for what seemed forever, although it seemed impossible for it to remain in that one spot. Then it let out an eagle screech, over and over again above me. I was rocked to my core, shaking and weeping in awe as I felt God's love and closeness all over me. He's really that awesome.

Chapter Two

RAISED FROM THE DEAD

BIKE RIDE TO HEAVEN

It was a few years later on another glorious spring day that I took off on a bicycle heading for Paonia, a town about 30 miles to the east. There's a long downhill stretch of pavement on the mesa with a great view; you can see all the way to the San Juan Mountains, some 90 miles to the south. As I flew down the road, I sat up straight and extended my arms out both sides like wings, glorying in the feeling of speed as the wind, sky, and earth whipped by. Suddenly I felt a wobble and looked down to see my front wheel completely disengage and come off. Everything seemed to be happening in slow motion, and I watched wide-eyed as the wheel propelled down the road, the front forks jammed into the blacktop, and I flew over the handlebars and slammed head first into the pavement. Upon impact, I kept right on going and left my body sprawled on the ground as I soared through a wavy tunnel of light to find myself in an incredible glowing place. The light was like the silver of moonlight and the gold of sunlight, but there was no moon or sun. I've tried to describe the scene, which I can still see vividly in my mind, but I can never do it justice. There was something like a classic Greek temple with tall columns in the background and a huge plaza by a placid lake surrounded by outrageously beautiful trees. I was in the plaza with a group of Ancient Ones, like Apostles or Prophets, and our communication was real and clear, though more telepathic than verbal. I found as we talked that I understood the wisdom of the ages, the plans and purposes for life and eternity. It was huge. I was there for hours, fascinated, enthralled, and could have stayed forever, but one of the Ancient Ones said I had to return. It was as if I dove back into that tunnel of light, and as I saw my crumpled body on the pavement, I heard a voice behind me say: "This one's gonna hurt!"

Bam! I hit my body with an impact that caused me to bounce up from the road into a sitting position. My mind was still as big as the universe, it seemed, and I could still remember all the wisdom of the ages, but there was the sure sense that it was slowly ebbing away. This was in 1975, and what pulled up right at that moment was a VW bus full of hippies, and a tall fuzzy-haired guy wearing overalls and no shirt came running across the road to me. The glory of another realm must have been all over my face like the wisdom was all over my mind, because he stopped in awe and said, "Man! You look psychedelic!" What I didn't realize was that there was also blood all over my face. Their goal was to get me medical help. My goal was to hold on to the wisdom of the ages.

18

I absolutely refused to go to a clinic, and as they were piling my trashed bike onto the roof, my goal included getting them to stop talking to me so I could ride this supernatural ebb tide of heavenly wisdom. I agreed to go with them to their house, because I knew there was a creek nearby, and I conceived a plan of sitting by the gently babbling water while I experienced the under-standing of the ages receding peacefully. I said something about water, which they misunderstood, and one of them took me into the house to a bathroom sink. Big mistake. I finally saw in the bathroom mirror what they had seen. I washed off some blood and begged them to take me to my house. They agreed, and I was immensely grateful be-cause it allowed me to spend the next few hours alone as I felt all of the wisdom and understanding slowly slip away. It was as if I were watching it all go, looking at and meditating on each item like a treasure or a great work of art in a gallery, as it passed by over a period of the next several hours. When it had all gone, the most horrendous concussion and headache moved in to take its place, and I lay on the floor of my house for two days in great pain. A neighbor had given us some homemade wine, and I drank the whole bottle in one night to try to calm the intense throbbing. Then on the third day I got up with no pain at all and went back out to work on the farm. I never did see a doctor or give the injuries another thought, but I've often reflected on that trip and what I'd seen and experienced. I've also never had any fear of death and have actually looked forward to seeing the other side again.

In the fall of 2008, over 30 years later, I had x-rays taken of my neck by a friend who is a chiropractor, and he exclaimed: "What happened to you? Did you get hit in the head with a baseball bat?!" The whole experience came back to me, and after looking at the x-rays I suddenly realized how unbelievably close I had come to death or paralysis and was able to fully comprehend the amazing protection God had placed on my life. But as I was talking to my wife about it, standing in our kitchen 33 years later, I had a revelation that I had been through death and back and that I had stepped into a new level of authority over death through that experience. Four times since then I have seen people come back from death when I've prayed for them. But those stories are for a later chapter.

READING THE BOOK

The group living on the farm had an eclectic mix of beliefs, from New Age to Spiritualism to Jesus, and we read a variety of esoteric literature. One day I picked up the bible for the first time; I plopped it open to the gospel of John, chapter 1, and I read:

"In the beginning was the Word,
and the Word was with God,
and the Word was God.
He was in the beginning with God.
All things were made through Him,
and without Him nothing was made.
In Him was life, and the life was the light of men.
And the light shines in the darkness,
and the darkness did not comprehend it."

I didn't have a clue what it meant, but it sounded mysterious and it stimulated my imagination. I decided to start at the beginning. Right away the book of Genesis grabbed me — partly because we were living outside in the creation and partly because we were farmers and could really appreciate the way God had made everything, "every grass and herb that yields seed according to its kind, and every tree that yields fruit, whose seed is in itself, according to its kind." But when I got to Abraham, it rocked my world.

God introduced Himself to Abraham and invited him to leave the world he knew to discover life with Him in a new place. God called Abraham His friend. *"I want to be Your friend, God."* And God led him to some land that Abraham didn't own and told him to live on it, and then gave him supernatural favor in the world and made some outrageous promises that Abraham could never have fulfilled on his own. God showed him the stars in the sky and the sand on the seashore and then spoke to him through them. It was so familiar; bells started ringing in me as I read those words on the farm He had given me that I didn't own. And he and Sarah lived in tents and had the child of promise by faith.

Linda and I were living in a tipi when she became pregnant with our first child. We rarely went to town and never to a doctor, because we were healthy, and because our whole lifestyle was focused on learning to relate to the Creator and living simply and interactively in the creation that He had made, and He'd made it to provide us extravagantly with everything we needed. While on a trip to town with another pregnant woman, Linda accompanied her on a visit to the County Health Nurse. Linda had experienced some spotting of a small amount of blood, so she asked him about it. He asked if he could check her, and when he did he told her frightening things about the placenta's being too low and possibly disengaging during childbirth so that the baby might die and Linda might bleed profusely. He filled her with fear regarding the birth of our baby, and she came home shaken and upset. I hugged her and we prayed and gave it to God. She went to our tipi to lie down, and as she prayed a perfect peace came over her from God that continued throughout the pregnancy.

We delivered our baby in our little home that I had just finished building, with no running water or electricity, with only the two of us there, and only a half hour of pain-less labor. As the full moon rose and bathed the world with its glow, we thanked God for being there for us and were grateful we'd believed in Him. As we lay down in bed with our tiny one between us, Linda said, "I think her name is Faith." And I was sure she was right. The child of promise by faith; this bible was coming alive for us.

In the weeks after the birth, as Linda looked into her baby's eyes, she realized that Faith couldn't see. We believed that God wanted to heal her. We prayed and sought books on healing, and it turned out that the little brick library in our small farm town had a section on spiritual healing. We brought home piles of books, and the interesting thing was that our favorite ones all talked about a group of people who believed together, prayed together, and saw God work miracles. *"Do you suppose there's a group like that around here?"*

Linda worked in an orchard raking up pruned branches for a woman who prayed with her workers every morning before sending them out. So Linda asked her about it. It turned out there was a group who met in town every Wednesday night and prayed and saw God do wondrous things. We went there one night with our babe in arms, and they welcomed us and drew us in and loved us. They sang beautiful songs with a guitar accompaniment, and we could feel the Presence of God fill the room. And they would all sing in different languages in beautiful harmonies, and then it seemed like choirs of other voices filled the room. How did they do that? And they would speak words of hope and promise and destiny and encouragement that came right from God and went right into our hearts. Sometimes they would say things that no one else could have known about us except for God; it was as if God were letting us know the answer to an issue we were concerned about. And they would tell of awesome things that God had done for and with them that week and what He was saying to them. I was fascinated.

But they kept mentioning the Blood, the Blood of Jesus, the Blood of the Lamb. I didn't really get that part, and it seemed kind of gruesome and not very spiritual or esoteric. But there was a lot about blood in the bible, too, and there were lots of animal sacrifices. What were all those sacrifices about? Even though I didn't understand it all, we kept going to those meetings and listening and asking questions and having wonderful experiences; we felt loved and accepted and adopted into a family. I loved that feeling. These people really knew Jesus and fully grasped the concepts of Lord and Savior. I figured "Lord" was like "Guru," but I realized I had no idea what the word "Savior" meant. What were we saved from? What are we saved for? What are we saved into? I really didn't know, so I asked Him.

It was April, and the earth smelled of springtime. There was still snow on the mountains and the sky was brilliant Colorado blue. We were living quite primitively at the time, and one day when I was hitchhiking down valley from Paonia, I became so caught up in the beauty of the creation that I just had to sing out to the Creator. I walked along the roadway praising Him, knowing He was right there and that He loved me. He was God and He loved me. What could be more amazing? Wasn't that salvation? I was overwhelmed by the Presence of Jesus. I stopped and I closed my eyes and felt His Presence all around me. Suddenly a great and overwhelming joy filled me until I felt as if I were overflowing with joy. When I could stand it no more, I walked on and was only beginning to think about hitchhiking when a big, shiny car stopped and a man in a tie leaned over, opened the door, and offered me a ride. I hopped in and he asked me: "Have you met Jesus?" I shuddered and looked back at the spot on the side of the road to see if He was standing there. I looked at the man and he said, "Have you accepted Him as your Lord and Savior?" He talked about how Jesus had died for my sins and he quoted the bible:

"If you confess with your mouth that Jesus is Lord,
and believe in your heart that God
has raised Him from the dead, you will be saved.
For with the heart one believes into righteousness;
and with the mouth confession is made into salvation.
For whoever shall call on
the name of the Lord shall be saved."

I just rode along in utter amazement.

So several nights later at the prayer meeting I cried out to Him, *"Be my Savior,"* and He said in my heart, "Let yourself be washed clean by the Blood of the Lamb. Don't hold on; let go. You can't figure it out. I took all the judgment you deserved and died for it. You're free. Just let yourself be washed clean by the Blood of the Lamb." So I did.

Maybe Niagara Falls would compare with what rushed over me and left me sitting there, sure and whole and spotless, full of something new inside. I felt that the Wisdom of the Ages was starting to creep back in, and my connection was getting stronger. It suddenly occurred to me that that was just what Jesus died for — to restore our connection to God, to the Father! And I remembered that first saying I had heard Him speak in that cabin in the mountains:

"I Am the Way, the Truth, and the Life.
No one comes to the Father except through Me."

I found out that those words were in the bible, right in the gospel of John, chapter 14.

THE BAPTISM IN THE HOLY SPIRIT

We were seeking healing for our daughter Faith, and our friends from the prayer group were faithful and encouraging. They took us to a Healing Conference in Grand Junction, which is the largest city in Western Colorado, though the population was less than 30,000 at the time. The conference was in a gymnasium and quite crowded. It was the largest group of people I'd been around in many years, and they were all enthusiastic and filled with joy, singing and clapping and dancing. I honestly don't remember any of the teachings, but after the first session we walked into the lobby where people were selling books and other items, and I was so full in my spirit that I couldn't relate to the scene. I found a room that was set aside for prayer and sat on the floor; I leaned

25

against a wall and closed my eyes and began to talk to God. All I wanted was more of Him. *"God, I want to know You more! You're all I want!"* I got more passionate and He came closer. Suddenly it seemed like I was in the middle of the sun in all its strength and brilliance, and everything else faded away; my entire being was engulfed by Him. It was ecstasy and intimacy maximized, and I was captivated. His love was filling me and I was breathless, overwhelmed by wave upon wave of glory and love and this amazing brilliance. I almost couldn't stand it, but at the same time I wanted more. I didn't know where I was and forgot about everything else. Radiance and brilliance and streaming chords of beautiful music crashed in wave after wave on the shore of my soul, and yet there was perfect peace. I never wanted to leave it.

Just then I felt a hand touch my shoulder and I opened my eyes to see a woman looking at me. I remember thinking: "How rude, this is really interrupting...." But I looked into her face and it was radiant, and suddenly I knew that she knew. "We need you over here," was all she said, and I got up and she led me across the room. I had never met anyone in the room before. An older woman was sitting in a chair with her back to me, and the first woman took my hands and placed them on the shoulders of the woman in the chair. All of a sudden I began to tell her about her life, how in 1949 she had rejected God because of an offense, and how He had been wooing her ever since. I told her many details about her life, and she burst into tears and begged forgiveness of God and gave her life to Him. She rose from the chair like a different person, and she and the first woman then sat a man down and placed my hands on his shoulders, and — BAM! — the same thing happened. This went on until it was time for the next session in the auditorium. I kind of floated out into the crowd and sat down with Linda and Faith. As soon as the session was over and it was time for a lunch break, the same two women came down the aisle with huge smiles on their faces and escorted me back to the prayer room. I stood there for the rest of the afternoon as people lined up to sit in the chair, and I told them many details of their lives and how much God loved them. People were healed on the spot, spiritually, mentally, emotionally, and physically. It felt like 220 volts of electricity were coursing through me as I laid hands on each one and spoke things I didn't know but that came to me and flowed through me, and sometimes I "saw" the details like a movie playing out before me. I'd never experienced anything like it before. Our friends from the prayer meeting came in, and later one of them said with joy and delight, "God sure used you today!"

But the next morning I was out in the fields again, irrigating, and my mind was filled with a whole slew of thoughts. I remember the scene perfectly. The sky was overcast and the day was breaking. Large beads of dew hung on the woven-wire fence where each wire crossed, like diamonds reflecting the light of the filtered morning sun, and my bare legs were wet with the dew from the tall grass. Thoughts crowded in and collided with each other in my mind. *"That didn't really happen. I just thought those things up." "Maybe I'm a man of God like the prophets in the bible." "Maybe I'm nuts." "How do I tell anyone about this? Will anyone believe it?"* I was overwhelmed with doubts and accusations, with pride and self-promotion, and I didn't seem to have any of the confidence and peace I'd felt so strongly only the day before. Did anyone understand what had happened?

MIRACLE IN A BLIZZARD

The only thing I did know was that I wanted more experiences like that, and I wanted more of life with God. I started telling people about Him and inviting everyone I knew to the Wednesday night prayer meeting. Many would come and they would receive comfort, words of encouragement, and real love and acceptance.

One winter night I'd brought a station wagon full of hippies to the prayer meeting. We were full of joy as we left the meeting, glowing with the experiences of the night. It had started snowing earlier, and we pulled onto the highway in a whiteout. I was watching for mailboxes and telephone poles along the right side of the highway just to stay on the road as we crept along in the blizzard. We all kept praying loudly, but I was especially focused because I felt responsible for this car full of young parents and small children. The snow was blowing sideways and I was searching for the next mailbox to appear through the snow and the darkness. *"Keep us safe, Lord,"* I prayed. I kept repeating the same prayer, when suddenly I was overwhelmed with the realization that He had been doing just that. We had been driving for 45 minutes or so and were all safe within the car and still on the road, even if we *were* creeping along at about five miles an hour. I thanked Him, and apologized for my doubts and fear.

"What would you have Me do for you?" I heard a voice in my head ask.

"Make the snow stop?" I questioned timidly.

That instant a few lagging snowflakes fell on the windshield, and then there were no more. The blizzard ceased in an instant and we were peering into black night.

28

I couldn't contain the flow of gratitude that poured forth. I felt completely wrapped up in a thick, strong love and tender care. How much this great and good God loves us!

SHIFTING THE ATMOSPHERE

I rarely went to town unless I really needed something, as the farm provided almost everything and in such a beautiful setting. But there were a lumberyard and a good hardware store and two variety stores in Delta, a town about half an hour from our home. One of the variety stores was run by really friendly people and the other by very crabby people. I was walking down the sidewalk past the crabby one, when I sensed the Lord's Presence and He asked me: "Where are you going?"

"To the variety store," I answered.

"Why, there's one right here," He said.

"Well, they're really crabby in this store. They're much friendlier at the one down the street." I replied.

"I'd like you to make this one a friendlier place by going in and being friendly. I want you to love them."

"Really? Okay." So I did. Every time I went to town. And the more I reached out to them and smiled and said encouraging things to them, the warmer it became. It took a little while, and I had to work at breaking through and getting the owners to actually look at me, and then I'd smile into the windows of their eyes and right down into their souls. It was great fun. And little by little I found them smiling back at me. At first it was tentative, sort of a half smile, but I responded to it so exuberantly that they'd look at each other and then back at me and then away. I

always wondered what they said to each other after I left. But before long they were greeting me with a smile when I entered, and the crabby place wasn't so crabby anymore.

God was teaching me about changing the atmosphere, but He was also teaching me about how love works. On two occasions I found myself working under rather tyrannical and extremely opinionated men, whom many people felt were impossible to work alongside. He picked me to work under them and then told me I wasn't to think a single negative thought while I was working with them. I lived with one of them for two weeks while we finished a job, and I found that because He had said to do it there was an impartation of His love and an empowerment to do what He'd asked that came along with the deal. I would have missed out on it if I'd resisted or complained. Instead, I got to learn three things.

First, I learned that strong and difficult people can also be amazing when you aren't afraid of them. These men began to respect me, and we had some great conversations and I found myself liking them, much to the surprise of some mutual associates. Second, I found that God imparts something of Himself to you when He asks you to do a difficult or even impossible task, and He gives you the strength to do it well, if you'll receive it. And third, I found that I can do anything He asks me to do. I even forgot to think about myself most of the time I was working on it!

320 MILES TO THE GALLON

We loved the farm where we worked from sunup to sundown and hardly ever went to town. I'd built our

30

small house on the creek, and Linda and I had raised our own food, been married there, and had our first child at home — I'd caught her as Linda gave birth in the full moon with only the two of us present. Life was good on the farm. Plowing and discing the earth was one of my favorite things to do. I felt I was part of some huge creation that was ongoing and would result in fruitfulness. But after we met Jesus and experienced the Holy Spirit, I found myself talking to Him as I spring-disced a fall-plowed field:

"I love working with tractors and the earth and seeds and plants and animals. But You delight in working with people. I feel this burning desire in my heart to work with people too, to watch people grow. What does that mean and what does it look like?" And I saw myself teaching in the public schools, planting seeds and nurturing their growth in the lives of young people. It seemed far-fetched.

Interestingly, though, that spring three different people who came to visit us on three different occasions said to me out of the blue: "You should be a teacher."

So that spring I hitchhiked the 200 miles to the State Teachers' College at Alamosa to check things out. They treated me like royalty. One department head said that a 29-year-old married man returning to school was like gold. So he gave me a job and helped me to get student aid. I found out the requirements for obtaining a Colorado teaching certificate and enrolled in 22 hours of credit, as I wanted to finish quickly. I was actually offered three part-time jobs for the fall semester and ended up teaching the freshman drafting class the next spring. When I got back to the farm we made plans for a major shift in our lives. A

31

friend offered me a job logging for the summer, which seemed an answer to our financial dilemma.

We must have looked like the "Beverly Hillbillies" or something out of "The Grapes of Wrath" as we drove into Alamosa, a college town, in my '48 Chevy flatbed truck with the homemade scrub-oak side racks. We were fresh off the farm for the fall semester, with everything we owned on that truck: a deep freeze full of chicken, beef, and veggies; cases of canning jars filled with green beans, tomatoes, and peaches; a mattress for a bed, a few boxes of clothes, and two rocking chairs tied way up on top. On the back 12 inches of space stood our two milk goats, Sunshine and Lily, who were securely strapped on, watching the world go by. Linda, eight months pregnant, sat looking out the passenger window, while two-and-a-half-year-old Faith played on the seat between us. We smiled and laughed as everyone stopped on the sidewalk to stare at us.

Moving my very pregnant wife from the home in the country she loved into the married-student dorms at Adams State College was an experience for which I'm grateful she's forgiven me. We went from hearing the peaceful sounds of crickets and nighthawks on the farm to being awakened after midnight on our first night in Alamosa by the screams of drunken students racing shopping carts through the parking lot outside our bedroom window. We sat up in bed and looked at each other, shook our heads and laughed. Our second daughter was born in our dorm apartment a month after we moved in, with only Linda, Faith, and me present. We named her Grace. And we were the talk of the college.

Unfortunately, the logger couldn't pay me, and I had

to quit two of the part-time jobs, as my growing family needed me. I felt that the Lord was showing me to prioritize my family and that He wanted me to make the right choice and trust Him. My work-study job and the loan paid for tuition and rent, and we had our food, but there was nothing left except $25 by the time we were all settled in.

"Lord," I said, *"This $25 won't really do much for us, and there's no hope of more coming in, so I'm going to give it to You and trust You for the rest. I think this was Your idea in the first place."* So I sent the money to someone who was doing a good work for Jesus and seeing people get healed.

We kept our goats four miles out of town at a friend's place and drove out to milk them every evening. It was Linda's piece of the country and peace of mind. But gas was $1.20 a gallon that year, and we watched the gauge go down to "E" and wondered how long it would last.

Somehow I'd gotten hold of a dollar, and I kept it in my pocket just in case I ever needed it. On a trip out to milk the goats on Empty, I sensed the Lord prompt me to put a dollar's worth of gas in the tank. I pulled into the station and opened the cap, shook the vehicle, and listened for any sound from the inside. Nothing. One dollar's worth. The gauge didn't even budge. I knew what kind of mileage I was getting, so I kept track of the trips. Four miles out and back, seven days a week. By the second week there was no way it should still be running.

Somehow I came up with another dollar, and I held on to it as tightly as the first. I was sure I'd be needing it sometime. Then I felt that prompting from the Lord again: "Put it in the tank."

Once again, nothing showed on the gauge. But we drove for several more weeks, and I picked up another dollar from somewhere and began to watch and listen expectantly. Three weeks. Then four. I'd see the gas station on the way to milk the goats and watch it as I drove by, waiting to hear His voice. I wouldn't do it unless He told me to. Always there would come from somewhere that single but amazing dollar, and always I would wait for that gentle prompting from the Lord.

The time between "fill ups" was increasing with each week. By winter we were getting 320 miles to the gallon! Then one day, with no sign of a dollar in sight, we received food stamps as part of our student loan. We couldn't trade them in for money, and we couldn't receive cash back as change from a purchase, but we were able to enjoy some specialty items from the grocery store, like ice cream and strawberries. I picked up some things there one day and was standing in the checkout line watching a difficult customer harass the cashier. When my turn came and I handed the cashier my food stamps she was a little harried, and the change was only 75 cents, so she said, "Here, just take it."

I stood there puzzled while little Faith pulled me by the hand out into the street, where I stood looking at the three quarters in my open hand and feeling as if my allowance had just been cut.

"Aw, God?" I thought as I pondered my situation. An old man walked down the pavement toward us just then, patted Faith on the head, reached into his pocket, pulled out a quarter and gave it to her. She reached up to me and placed it in my hand with the other three. Yes! We're back in the game.

It went like that through the fall and into the winter, and it became a delight to see where the dollar would come from and to wait to hear the awesome voice of the Lord who loves us tell us when it was the right time to "put it in the tank." He kept stretching it out as He was stretching us! So later that winter when my logging buddy finally paid me the thousands of dollars he owed me, it was like saying goodbye to an old friend as we left the era of the one-dollar bill and the empty gas tank we'd grown to love. The Lord was introducing us to His amazing ways, and this was just the beginning, as His love has led us into many adventures of Faith, and by His Grace He has taken us places we never knew we could go. He's proven Himself to be completely trustworthy. And we have learned, at least a little bit, how to listen and obey.

GRACE IS HEALED

When we moved to Alamosa Linda was eight months pregnant. We moved from an idyllic home that I had built on a small creek on the farm — something between an earthship, a greenhouse, and a hobbit hole — into the married-student dorms at Adams State College. Something of a shock. It was autumn, so we had stacks of bushel boxes of fruit outside our door while we canned. We often left the door open, and the smell of fresh bread baking from our own home-grown wheat drove everyone crazy. We were already an oddity, but when Linda had our baby in our dorm apartment attended only by Faith and me, we topped the charts. I was even invited to speak to

35

the Psychology classes on "alternative lifestyles."

I was in the kitchen boiling water to sterilize string to tie off the umbilical cord when I heard her name clearly.

"I think her name is Grace," I called out to Linda as she nursed her newborn in the bedroom.

"It is. I've known that all along," she replied. I'd been hoping for a boy and come up with a fantastic array of wild boy names, but never thought of one for a girl, so she was way ahead of me.

Grace was having a little trouble breathing, so Linda used a Delee suction to get the mucus out of her nose. The tube went into the right nostril easily, but the left seemed plugged. The more we tried the more it seemed there was solid blockage, like bone, that was impassable. We'd been in Denver Children's Hospital a month earlier and met a small child who had solid bone in her nose that had to be drilled out, and she had gasped and wheezed and snorted and cried a lot. We had to pray that scene out of our thoughts. However, we decided to go to a doctor first thing in the morning to have Grace checked.

It's an experience trying to explain yourself to a medical professional when you've just had your baby at home alone. This doctor was pretty cool, though. He tried the Delee in the right nostril and it worked. The left nostril was still blocked. He tried three times and began to give us varying forms of bad news, when I said:

"How 'bout if we all pray together and you try one more time?" He was agreeable. I prayed a straightforward prayer, just long enough to feel the Presence of God. Then all eyes were on him as he placed the tube in her nose.

36

Voila! It slid right in without any resistance at all!

"That's incredible!" he said. "It was obviously blocked."

"It's a miracle," I replied. He agreed, and all of us praised God together!

When we returned to the dorms in the morning with our newborn, a woman exclaimed:

"You had your baby! Did they let you out of the hospital so soon?"

"She was born right here in our bedroom last night." We were the talk of the campus, but Grace was healed and God got the credit!

ANOTHER BLIZZARD MIRACLE

My parents flew out for Thanksgiving to meet the baby and stayed at my sister Sally's house in Paonia, and we drove up from Alamosa for the holidays. Thanksgiving in Colorado always seems to bring the first big snowstorm of the season and is the worst time to travel. After driving for four hours in a whiteout we finally made it to Gunnison, which was only about halfway there. We stopped and ate and prayed again. By then it was dark. We'd been loudly singing songs of praise as we inched along, and as we left Gunnison we caught up to a snow plow and followed it and its lights and clearly plowed swath to the top of the first pass. Then we sang even louder and thanked God for this great favor. As we began to climb Cerro Summit, I said aloud:

"God, You've been so good to us. If there's anyone

we can help out, show us."

Within minutes I noticed through the darkness and the falling snow that there were taillights way down off the road in the ravine. I stopped the car and got out and slid-climbed down the embankment through the deepening snow until I reached the car, a big older Pontiac sedan with only highway tires. Inside there was a young mother with her baby.

"Can you pull me out?" she pleaded. I looked up at our trusty Volkswagen station wagon.

"Not likely." And then I heard myself say, "But I'll tell you what I'm going to do. I'm going to get behind you and push with my body and God is going to take you up onto the road. You just put it in gear and go with it."

She looked skeptical and hopeful at the same time. Is that possible? I went around to the back and looked up the steep snowy embankment.

"Okay, God." I leaned into the back of the car and started to push and it took off so fast that I had to run, stumbling through the deep snow on the steep hillside trying to keep up! When the car was up on the road it stopped, and when I arrived panting at the driver's side she opened the window and with wide eyes exclaimed: "HE DID IT!!" He sure did. I got in my car and followed her until we came down out of the high country and into Montrose, where the snow lightened up. He's so involved!

LET'S GET HIGH AND READ THE BIBLE

The more we experienced the miraculous ways that God was working in our lives, the more we talked to friends about it. We were living in an era when upper-, middle-, and lower-class educated young people were going "back to the land" in an attempt to reconnect with the basics of life: earth, fire, water, air. We were thriving on the adventure of growing our own food, cutting wood to build fires for heating and cooking, hauling our water, and breathing clean air. We camped in tipis on the earth and then built our own houses with wood, stone, and adobe. And we were all hungry for some spiritual reality. Psychedelics such as peyote and psilocybin mushrooms were common; smoking home-grown marijuana was rampant. Celebrations with all of the above and musical instruments around a campfire were corporate religious experiences. Literature from every eastern and native religion was devoured, and folks were trying to develop and walk out their own hybrid strains of spiritual reality. The bible was an unread curiosity, and "Jesus is just all right with me." He was pretty universally accepted as an avatar, but not really well known in a personal and intimate way. So our new Jesus journey elicited curiosity from some of our friends and neighbors.

After we moved back to the farm from Alamosa, I remember the first time we invited a diverse group of individuals over for a discussion in our back yard. The topic I wanted to explore was: "What is your concept of God?" Diverse pretty well covers it. But I was looking for those who could express some kind of real experience they'd had with God and were open to encountering Him and might be interested in reading and exploring the bible together. There were a few who were interested that God seemed to be drawing us to, as well as some who had started coming to the Wednesday night prayer meeting in town. And so began our Saturday morning bible study.

None of us had ever actually *studied* the bible, and though I was reading it and *experiencing* it, I knew practically nothing. So we jumped in to the gospel of Matthew and read it out loud, verse by verse, and asked questions and discussed it, and when we had no idea what a passage meant, we prayed and asked the Holy Spirit to give us understanding. And it worked! We kept at it for several years, and I remember our delight as ideas, inspiration, creativity, and wisdom were shared by each one of us. It was a joyous time of discovery and it spurred me to dive in and research the scriptures myself. I spent a lot of time that summer immersed in the bible, comparing different books in the Old and New Covenant, and falling in love with the God who was showing us a huge, Divine master plan. We bought our first gigantic *Strong's Exhaustive Concordance of the Bible* that year, which referenced every word in the bible and gave its definition, and it doubled as a booster seat for our young kids at the dinner table.

One Friday night I slept outside with Faith and Grace in the thick green grass of our lawn that stretched from the back porch to the garden. Linda, nine months pregnant, woke us at five a.m. to tell us she was in labor. The excitement began. Both the girls had been born at home with no one else present, but we'd planned this one to be different. I called a lady friend who lived across the road, as well as my cousin Paul, who was living on the farm in a tipi, and a teenage girl we loved who came and photographed the birth. That girl later became a midwife and eventually married my cousin and now they have nine children of their own!

Our first son, Jesse, arrived at around seven a.m. in

40

our little house on the farm. His sisters were part of the birth, and we all celebrated together the miracle of new life. My own sister Sally arrived as we were all taking turns holding him, and then at 9:00 the bible study group showed up to find us with a new baby. By that time we'd completely forgotten it was Saturday. The celebration increased, but we never got into the scriptures that day. There was something about the miracle of childbirth and the radiance that fills the atmosphere after a birth that gave a glimpse into the new life that lay ahead of us as our journey continued to unfold.

Chapter Three

100% COMMITMENT

THAT BOY IS DEAD

When we returned to the farm in 1981, I began teaching in the Delta County schools. I was driving my '48 Chevy pickup down Highway 65 from Cedaredge one afternoon and I passed through the tiny town of Eckert. Fruit orchards and spring flowers graced both sides of the highway. Suddenly old movies started to play in my head, showing me scenes from the past of ugly things I had done and ugly ways I had been. I shuddered at the thoughts, not sure what to do with them. Just then the voice of the Holy Spirit spoke to me: "That boy is dead. It's a sad story, but he's dead. That isn't who you are anymore. You're a new creation now, a whole new man."

And I believed Him. I decided it was the truth. *"I AM a new man!"* And I began to look into and explore who that new man was instead of thinking about the old one. I've never regretted that decision.

FULL MOON ON HART'S BASIN

Not long after that I was alone in the late-night darkness, driving through the Surface Creek Valley up to the farm on Redlands Mesa. It was a spring night and the moon was full. As I drove past Hart's Basin I saw that a huge flock of migrating sandhill cranes had landed at the lake. The whole scene, gloriously lit by moonlight, was breathtaking, and I had to stop and get out. Something of the Glory of the Creator and His creation completely overtook me. I stood by the silhouetted trees at the water's edge and drank in the beauty of the full moon in a clear sky and its reflection on the water, scattered across a thousand ripples. Many hundreds of birds were highlighted in soft moonlight, casting rippled moon shadows on the purple and blue surface of the shallow lake. Scattered among the grey-brown sandhills were a few dozen whooping cranes. Their snowy white feathered bodies shone brilliantly in the moonlight, and they stood out like a small scattering of bright lights flung across the water, spread out as they were throughout the greater grey-brown flock. Wow.

I began to praise God with increasing intensity. I came to a place of complete surrender, where I felt I gave myself to Him at a level I'd never experienced before. My life wasn't my own anymore; it seemed I only wanted to live life in Him and with Him and for Him and through Him. And the other way around, too — I in Him and He in me. *"Fill all of me with all of You, Lord."* I felt like the God of the universe, the Imaginer of all creation, was pulling on me, calling me. I couldn't resist and didn't want to. I made a greater commitment to Him and felt everything in and around me step up a notch. I told Him I wanted my whole life to be a full-time ministry to Him. It was a covenant in the moonlight, as if the moon were a witness to a solemn oath. And I felt as if He received me in some deeper way as the son that He loves, affirmed me, and embraced me. The connection just got stronger and I crossed a threshold from which there was no turning back; Heaven was completely open, and I stepped in. I was drawn to Him like my eyes were drawn to the scene. Looking back now, it seems that He was highlighting me, delighting in me, like the moon delighted in the snowy white whooping cranes that shone so brightly reflecting its light as they stood out in the midst of the huge but muted flock of grey-brown sandhill cranes.

BREAKDOWN ~ SHIFT HAPPENS

Things got really crazy after that. I was teaching at Hotchkiss High School and living on the farm on Redlands Mesa, so I had a long drive off the mesa and down Leroux Creek, and then down into the North Fork Valley, through town and across the river to school each day. The first thing that happened was that our car broke down, and when I went to tow it home with our trusty '48 Chevy truck I had a flat tire way out on a country road as it was getting dark. I never lost my peace, though, and I can remember thanking God that at least it wasn't raining. Then the Chevy died as well. It was spring, and time to till the garden, so the rototiller and lawn mower broke down next. The washing machine followed, and then a few other items. I think the ice cream maker kept working.

Getting to school became difficult, so my neighbor offered to lend me his Jeep. On the way back from school it died and I had to get a student to help me tow it home.

Another friend offered his car the next day, which also died on the way home. For a week I drove to school in a different vehicle each day, and the kids asked in wonder: "How many cars do you have?!" A series of them broke down so consistently that I hesitated to borrow anything. One day I showed up in an unmuffled and very loud, red, oxidized and very rusty older Ford Falcon convertible with large "JESUS" stickers all over it. As I pulled past the front of the school, all my boys were outside and the very loudest yelled over the din of the car: *"What is THAT??!!"* It died at the grocery store on the way home.

The next morning was bright and sunny. I was in the front yard communing with God about how I would get to school, when a woman who lived several miles away, whom I barely knew, pulled into the drive. I was way past asking to use anyone's vehicle, but she asked me what was happening in my world, so I told her I needed to get to school (thinking maybe she was going that way), and she said, "If you'll take me home, you can take my car." I gave her fair warning. It was a brand new car, too. The kids thought it was the nicest one yet.

It made it home that day without a hitch. But the next morning was a crucial turning point in facing the opposition head-on. I'd been functioning at such a high level of Grace and Peace since that night at Hart's Basin that it felt like nothing could ever shake it. But that remarkable state of favor I'd been experiencing was being severely challenged. Is this what happens when you get serious? Is it worth all this hassle? What did I really believe about God? I felt I was in a face-off — not with God, but with the overwhelming circumstances. Everything was being tested. I remember sharing the perplexity of the situation with a friend who had been walking this journey longer than I had. I explained the situation in all its bewildering and humorous detail and waited for the compassion to come.

"Well, they killed the apostles, you know." That was it. Not what I'd expected. But I got the point that opposition is real, especially to a commitment and covenant and promise that opens Heaven and points down the road toward a destiny.

I stood in the front yard that morning and said, *"Lord, I know You gave me this job and I've given You my life and everything in it. Something's messing with Your stuff. This job and these kids are my assignment, and I know You gave them to me. I'm confident that You are committed to me and to the things that concern me, like this job and getting there on time. So I'm going to be completely ridiculous and I'm just going to start walking down the road, and though it's physically impossible for me to get there on time walking the 15 or so miles, I know it's gonna happen, even if You have to transport me or stop the day like You did for Joshua in the bible. So let's just walk down this road together and see how it plays out."*

At first I started praising Him and thanking Him. But soon I began to feel convicted in my heart of all kinds of arrogance and pride. I broke down before Him and began weeping as I walked, confessing, repenting, crying, thanking. By the end of five miles I was drained and refilled.

I looked at my watch. *"You're going to have to do something really fast, Lord."* No one drove off this mesa in this direction at this time of day. There wasn't a car on the road. I was walking along praising Him when I began to hear a very faint engine sound. As it got louder, I recognized the unmistakable roar of a Harley Davidson motorcycle. Getting closer. I continued to walk. The guy on the bike pulled up and asked, "Need a lift? Where you headed?"

He wasn't going out by the high school, but he said he'd be glad to take me. "Strangest thing, though," he said, "I wasn't really going out at all, but I suddenly got this strange urge to hop on my bike and head toward Hotchkiss." I smiled real big. *Thanks*. We pulled up to the front of the school just as the bell rang.

And everything broke that day. Not my stuff, but the opposition and harassment. There was a shift in the entire atmosphere. The stuff actually *stopped* breaking and I began to put it all back together with a great amount of ease. A friend who was a Volvo mechanic came and worked on my car for trade. The garden got tilled and planted and life went on. And I knew even better Who the Greater One is.

HORDES OF GRASSHOPPERS

That summer more miracles broke out. An interesting one involved crops. We still raised all our vegetables, now in the smaller quarter-acre garden by the house, and we canned and froze what we needed to get through the winter. But that year a grasshopper plague swept across the mesa, and they stripped plants bare of their leaves, eating up whole harvests. I was watching them move toward our fields in a huge black wave, and I talked to the Lord about it. One morning I was reading the book of Malachi in the bible, and when I got to chapter three, something rose up inside me as I read these words from verses 10 and 11:

> *"Bring all the tithes into the storehouse,*
> *that there may be food in My house,*
> *and **prove Me** now in this," says the LORD of hosts,*
> *"If I will not open for you the windows of heaven*
> *and pour out for you such blessing*
> *that there will not be room enough to receive it.*
> *And I will **rebuke the devourer** for your sakes,*
> *so that **he will not destroy the fruit of your ground**,*
> *nor shall the vine fail to bear fruit for you in the field,"*
> *says the LORD of hosts.*

"I tithe, Lord. So You're telling me to prove You in this! Okay." And I went out into the garden and told it to the grasshoppers. And I told it to the thief, the devourer who is behind all the devouring, robbing, and destruction. And I praised the One who came that we would have Life and Life More Abundantly. And I felt great when I left the garden that night. The next morning I was excited to go out and see that the grasshoppers were completely gone. The only problem was that they weren't. They were thick across the garden, like a dark shadow. But as I looked more closely, I noticed that they were not eating a thing. The corn was in tassel and the tomatoes were red on the vine, and they were all covered with grasshoppers, but there was NO destruction. The grasshoppers were traveling across the plants without even taking a bite! And it continued that way until they moved westward, off the property. We had NO grasshopper damage in the garden at all. I figured that He proved that one pretty well, and

that He's really faithful like He says!

ARTHRITIS HEALED

We were part of a church family in Cedaredge at this time, and I kept hearing God speak to me in the meetings. Sometimes it was for the whole group of people, sometimes for one person, and sometimes just for me. I was learning how to listen and respond. I remember one time Linda and I were sitting in the front row with our three young kids and a couple of neighbors' kids when the Lord downloaded a message for the whole group. There were a few minutes of silence, so I spoke out what I was hearing while attempting to contain several children including our youngest, one-year-old Jesse, who was climbing all over me. When I finished, Linda smiled, applauded, and said, "Good job!"

One morning I heard the Lord tell me to pray for a woman and He would heal her. There was a call for prayer and people went to the front of the room to be prayed for. I walked up, looking for the woman God would heal. I sensed nothing, so I went to an older woman and prayed for her, but nothing noticeable happened. Then I saw another woman and was drawn to her. I went over and touched her and immediately her arms shot up and she started crying out. We both burst into tears at the same moment. Instantly God had healed her; she had been experiencing intense arthritic pain in her hands and arms that had gotten worse each year. She is an artist, and she had been having trouble even holding a brush. When I saw her 20 years later the arthritis pain had not returned, and she was teaching painting as well as putting on her own shows. *God, You are so good.*

CANCER HEALED

Shortly after that there was a call for healing prayer during one of the morning meetings. I remember that it was very specific: "God is here to heal. If you come forward you WILL be healed." I stayed in my seat praying and listening. Then I heard God tell me to go to an older man sitting in a section near the middle of the building and pray for him. I actually argued a little, saying, *"Lord, You said if we **come forward** You will heal us."* There was a silent pause, and I knew I'd better catch the wind of the Spirit while it was blowing, so I got up and sailed around the side to the back of the building. I didn't know this man, but he was in the "old folks" section, and right in the middle of a row filled with people on both sides of him. I took a deep breath and climbed over two rows of people, coming upon him from behind. He was leaning forward, so the only thing I could do was lunge over the back of the pew and wrap my arms around him from behind. He handled it pretty well. I began to pray whatever the Spirit gave me, and he began to sob. After a while I felt I was finished, so I turned around and tried to navigate my way back out of there while people were returning from prayer up front. It was a little trickier to get out, as the seats were filling up, but I managed.

A few days later I ran into him and he told me his story. A year earlier his wife had died of cancer. He had taken her home and nursed her through all her pain and she had died at home. He had recently been to the doctor and just learned that he now had cancer and they suspected that it was malignant. He was overwhelmed, as he'd been through his wife's pain with her, and now he was alone to face it all again. He said that when I'd prayed for him he felt hope rise up in him. He'd gone back to the doctor, who could find no trace of the cancer! *Thank you, Mighty and Loving God!*

KNOCKING ON DOORS

Around this time I began to feel a very great desire to knock on everyone's doors and tell them about Jesus and His amazing Kingdom that affects every aspect of life in this world. I didn't know anyone who did this sort of thing and wasn't sure I could pull it off with any amount of composure or finesse. As I was praying about it, I received an impression that I should call a man I barely knew who was part of a very conservative church. He was good at talking to people about anything and would be great at this sort of thing, I was certain.

"Ken, I have this great desire to knock on people's doors and tell them all about Jesus."

"Praise the Lord!" was his enthusiastic reply. "How 'bout next Thursday evening?"

This began an adventure that lasted for several years. I had many other partners, and we covered eleven towns in five adjoining counties of Western Colorado. But it started with Ken, and as the doors we knocked on were opened to us, we would be asked what church we were from. When we'd answer that we were from two different churches, it always dumbfounded people and they would want to know why we were doing this together — that opened the way for us to tell them that it's not about the church; it's all about Jesus.

My cousin Paul and I later decided to do our door

knocking on Saturday mornings, and one of us would call up the other and ask, "You want to go today?"

"I dunno, do you?" And then we'd resolve it by convincing each other that if we'd just get out there we'd have an amazing time. And we always did. There are lots of stories I can tell about those adventures, but the thing that is outstanding to me is that He had given me such an overwhelming desire to do something I absolutely would *never* have done on my own. Someone once asked me if I was just doing it as a work out of my own flesh or desire, and I could assure him that there is no way that *my* flesh was *ever* going to knock on doors to talk to total strangers about anything. It was all a work of God.

THE AMAZING DELIVERANCE
OF A NAVAJO MAN

For six years the church we were part of kept growing. For the last three years we experimented with huge musical dramas in the spring, right before the celebration of the death and resurrection of Jesus. I became Jesus for those three productions, nightly being nailed to a cross and then gloriously rising from the dead, complete with strobe lights and dry-ice smoke and clouds. It became so intense that I would arrive a couple of hours early and lie face down at the foot of the cross and weep on the dark stage as I thought of all He went through for me. During the dramas people would have encounters with Him, and some were even healed. The songs were very stirring, and my cousin Paul sang the lead with great passion and anointing, backed by a whole choir.

The church decided to take a team to Phoenix,

Arizona, to attend a conference put on by a mega-church that conducts huge dramatic spectacles and see what we could learn. On the second day of the conference, we had the afternoon off and I was downtown by the rescue mission. I sat on the curb by a bus stop talking to some homeless people, and I invited them to an outreach the church was holding that night where there would be free food, and a rock musician and a sports hero would share their stories about how they had met Jesus and He had affected their lives. Some of the guys were willing to come along, and one Navajo man seemed interested but struggled to make up his mind. He had a really hard time speaking but finally explained that if he wasn't back here at 6:00 p.m. he wouldn't get a bed. I heard myself promise him I'd find him a place to sleep.

We caught a bus headed toward the church, and I found myself engaged in a conversation with an older man seated directly behind the Navajo man. As we got into a discussion about the bible, I started to read some verses from the New Testament to him. Each time I would read a verse, the Navajo man would grab his head dramatically and groan and make very loud noises. So I read another and watched him. Sure enough. Slowly he turned his head around and looked right at me. He was a large man with a really huge head.

"What is that book?" he roared. This could have been intimidating, but I felt a great peace and was really drawn to the man.

"It's the bible," I replied. "What's happening?" And I moved up into the seat right next to him.

He began to explain that he had been drunk for so

54

long that he could no longer think. He had awakened that morning with a strange awareness that if he drank again that day he would die. When I had found him he was sitting on the curb trying to make some sense of it all, but felt unable to think or move. I'd been the first person to try to talk to him, so he had come along on the bus but didn't really know why. His brain just wasn't working.

"When you read those words, my brain starts to work again." He spoke slowly and deeply.

"Really?" I tried it again and looked at him.

He jerked like an electric shock was arcing through his brain. I picked some especially good verses. More jolts and jerks, and then he started to talk more clearly and explain how he felt with much more lucidity. As the bus drove on I continued to read to him and watched and smiled, and he became clearer and clearer. It was almost like the world was making sense to him. Until we got to the church.

It was a huge church that seated over 5,000 people. We were late, and as we entered on the ground floor near the front, all we could see were thousands of people filling every seat in the entire auditorium. We were both overwhelmed, and I pulled him along by the arm up the aisle toward the back of the immense building. I saw the two friends I was traveling with and introduced him, but they had no extra seats. He was a little zombie-like, and their eyebrows raised a bit as they smiled at me. We ended up being ushered to the elevator and up to the third-level balcony. My friend was way out of his comfort zone.

The show was dramatic and professional, and the heroes shared some awesome stories. When the preacher spoke it was obvious that he was an anointed evangelist, and as he called out to people to come to Jesus there was definitely an experiential pull to go forward and surrender everything to God. People began to fill the aisles as they moved to the front. I looked at Leonard, my new friend. He was totally gone, like a zombie for sure. The preacher made a series of pleas, but Leonard was locked up tight. It seemed that the preacher had already made his last call, but he was persistent and called out one more time. I got right in Leonard's face and asked him if he would go forward if I would go up with him. He grunted and gave a sharp jerky nod that looked like yes. So I got up.

He was like a walking dead man and moved so slowly it looked as if his feet and even his whole body were filled with lead. We had to get to the elevator first, and then down to the main floor. I thought we'd never get there. As we plodded down to the front, there were already many people coming back. We finally made it to a bench up front where Leonard dropped to his knees and buried his head in his hands. I looked around, and everybody had left by this time. I took out my little pocket bible and read a couple of verses of hope and God's love and plan to Leonard. He melted, and I led him in some words of surrender. Then I just sat there as Leonard did business with Jesus and Jesus did His stuff.

A few minutes later Leonard looked up at me with an outrageous smile on his face and stood up beaming. He looked totally transformed.

"You doing okay?" I asked. He hugged me!

We started walking up the aisle as the meeting was ending and people were beginning to move out of their seats. I found my friends, and they stared wide-eyed as Leonard smiled and beamed at them. "He doesn't look like the same guy you came in with!"

Leonard was hungry, and the homeless were being fed outside; as I led him out to get food I remembered my promise to find him a place to sleep. I asked the outreach pastor if the church had any facilities, but he said no. He wasn't very encouraging about taking a homeless Navajo man home, and I realized I had to make a decision. So I prayed and then asked my friends, "What do you think about Leonard staying in the motel room with us?" They were princes and agreed, so we took him along.

A shower sounded like heaven to him. Our budget motel had two queen beds, and while Leonard was in the bathroom we decided I would sleep with him and my two buddies would take the other bed. Leonard came out and flopped on the bed and declared, "I can't stop smiling!" We smiled and talked and laughed so hard we almost cried, staying up half the night, totally intoxicated with the Holy Spirit. He was a completely new creation. He told us that taking the walk down to the front of the building had been the hardest thing he'd ever done in his life. "I felt like my shoes were filled with lead and I was trying to walk through quicksand and that all the power in the world was pulling me back. I couldn't have done it without your help."

I wanted to take him back to Colorado with me. We all went out to breakfast and then to the morning meetings at the church. I got Leonard into a class on evangelism and discipleship, and I introduced him to some people on staff at the church. It was all very new to him. When it was time for us to leave, I felt the Lord clearly tell me to drop him off downtown. Leonard was fine with that, and as I left him I felt I was placing him in the hands of Jesus. He later wrote and told me he had a job at the airport and was doing well, and I sent him some good reading material. We lost contact soon after that, but I have to believe that the God who could reach into his darkness and bring him out into fullness of joy can take care of him forever. And He can. And He does.

I CAN'T HEAR YOU, GOD

Since the time I'd first met Jesus, I had been experiencing an uncanny ability to hear God speak to me. This ability was available to me all the time and in any situation — it might manifest in a prophetic word about someone's destiny, wisdom in making an important group decision, a word of knowledge about someone's past, or even insight into how to repair a mechanical conundrum. It especially came in handy in problem situations that needed a solution. I've had Him tell me the whereabouts of a septic tank no one could find, the location of the break in a water main, and how to extricate a starter motor from the Japanese puzzle of an old Toyota truck without having to unbolt all the surrounding pieces. But when we left the church in Cedaredge to attend a small church in Hotchkiss, it seemed that the well had dried up.

Our Cedaredge church family had blessed our departure and sensed it was clearly the right move for us. I was teaching at the high school in Hotchkiss and reaching out to the students there, and we wanted to be involved with a group of people who lived and worked in that community. The young church was growing and miracles of God's love were happening; people were meeting Jesus and their lives were being transformed, and many dramatic healings were taking place. But soon after we started meeting with the group in Hotchkiss, it seemed I couldn't hear God say anything. It was strange. I'd wait quietly in His Presence, pray, and even fast, but I got nothing. When we'd all feel His Spirit moving in a meeting I'd listen patiently, but again, nothing. *"What's happening, Lord?"* No answer.

I opened the bible one day and began to read. Suddenly I sat up and spoke to the Lord: *"God, I love hearing Your voice. I love the things You say to me and to others through me. But if You don't ever speak to me again through any kind of utterance, I'm going to listen to You through Your word. It says that men of old wrote it as they were moved by the Holy Spirit. It says it's not the words of men, but 'in truth the word of God which effectively works in us who believe.' It says You inspired it and that those men wrote down the very mind and heart of God. So if I can't hear You speak Your will to me, I'm going to search it out in the scriptures. I'm just going to dig out everything You've said on a matter and find Your will."* So I did. I began to study the scriptures with renewed zeal, and through them the Wisdom of the Ages came alive again for me.

One of the things I read at this time was something Jesus said in the gospel of John, chapter 15: "If you love Me, keep My commandments." *"I really love You, Lord. What are Your commandments?"* I wasn't really interested in the Ten Commandments, good as they are, because I understood about *covenant*, and knew from His word that I am under a New Covenant. The Old one was all about the Law and what the standard of *righteousness* was. No one could attain that righteousness on his own, so there was a whole sacrificial system; our failure to be righteous resulted in the death of an animal. It seemed the punishment for everything was death; every sin and failure resulted in death — somebody's blood was poured out. We worked really hard to be good, and when we failed we had to work out a sacrifice. It was a real performance religion, under the Law. But then Jesus came and changed everything. Suddenly *righteousness* became a *Gift!* How good is that?! When we fail, the sacrifice for our wrongdoing has already been made; *His blood* was poured out when He died for us. His righteousness is now a *Gift* no matter what we do. He said it's a *better* covenant, a covenant of *Grace*. That's a word I had to do a lot of research on. It seems it has to do with the absolutely amazing favor God shows toward us to give us such a gift as righteousness when we really have not earned it. And then the word *Grace* includes the empowerment He gives us to walk in the righteousness of Jesus. That's completely mind-boggling! We suddenly receive everything Jesus deserves. So where sin is in abundance, more Grace is poured out! And Paul's age-old question in Romans chapter 6 remains: "Shall we continue to sin so that grace might abound?" Figure that one out.

So my research entailed finding out what Jesus meant when He said, "If you love Me, keep My commandments." It wasn't about performance, obviously. But what, then? I knew that His Love had so thoroughly captivated me and filled me that I could only love Him back. So the "if" part was irrelevant, but "keep" could be important. The New Covenant was written in Greek, so I looked up the definition of the Greek word used here. It's a verb that means: *to attend to carefully, to watch over, to observe, to give heed to, to guard, to take care of, to hold fast.* So if I'm going to do that, I need to know what He commands. It was Jesus who was talking, so I decided to look up everything He commanded. My bible had red print wherever Jesus spoke, so that was helpful. I went through all the red and underlined everything He said in the imperative mood. Remember grammar? It's a verb in a command form: "Do this, go there, say this ...."

My underlining began to cover pages. But I started to see patterns and repetitions. I took out paper and made columns on it, then wrote down the number of times He gave the same command. Some of them He said over 20 times! I knew that the ones He spoke most often weren't necessarily the most important commands He gave, but I figured that He spoke them so often because perhaps we needed to hear them the most. Perhaps there was a lot of opposition in life that made them important to hear over again, and we would really need to remember those words to face the obstacles in life. I discovered there were three commands He gave more than all the rest. These were repeated 18 to 28 times. I found that the third most frequently spoken command of Jesus is "Fear not." That is followed closely by the second most frequently spoken command: "Believe." But the number-one command amazed me. It came in many forms, but they all said the same thing. I grouped them together because of their similarity and found that they were a huge part of His vocabulary. The number-one command of Jesus, in frequency of times spoken, is "Be made whole!" Sometimes He'd say "Be healed" or "Rise up and walk," but it was always the same intent; He was commanding *Wholeness.* I realized that's why He came to us. He came to reconcile us to wholeness, which is how God created us and intended for us to function. So I decided, because I loved Him, that I would *attend to carefully, watch over, observe, give heed to, guard, take care of, hold fast to* **Not Fearing**, but **Believing**, and in all ways receive His Grace to **Be Made Whole**! He tells us later in His word that His commands are not burdensome. His outstanding ways make me love Him even more! And in His great love for me, He started speaking to me again. He told me He hadn't been withdrawing from me, He had been wooing me, drawing me to press in to Him. It worked, and His word through the bible became even more alive to me as it showed me many more aspects of His character, love, wisdom, and goodness.

BRAIN TUMOR HEALED

While I was teaching at Hotchkiss High School, I asked the principal if I could hold a bible study for students before school. He was a Catholic man, and his mother-in-law was part of that wild Holy Ghost prayer meeting where we had first met Christian believers. He was very open, so he talked to the superintendent and they gave me permission.

I taught high school Shop, and many of my students were struggling in their academic classes. They were a pretty rowdy lot, but I really loved them and they felt it. Most of them knew almost nothing about the bible. I invited them all to a bible study at 7:00 on Wednesday mornings, right before school. I was actually amazed that so many of them showed up! We went through the gospel of Matthew, chapter by chapter, and read challenging things for teenage boys to ponder — like how lusting after a woman is the same as committing adultery with her.

62

That one was a hit. We had some great, raw, and real conversations. I told them that we could study about Jesus all we wanted, but there would come a time when they would have to decide if they wanted to MEET Him, because that's where it all starts to really happen. They'd ask questions like: "Can I meet Jesus and still party?" And I'd suggest: "Why don't you meet Him and then ask Him if He wants to go to that party with you?" One boy didn't come back after that.

It became really fun as they began to get hungrier, and one by one a boy would come to me and ask if he could meet Jesus. We'd check our schedules, and often it would be after sports practice in the afternoon. We'd go into the trailer by the shop where a classroom and my office were located. I'd tell them we'd better sit down, and then I'd pray and the Holy Spirit would come and whack us both. We'd be out for about 20 minutes, and then the boy would come up wide-eyed and say something like: "Whoa ...." Or one time: "Wow. Now I have a *purpose* in my life!" For years after that I would see those kids and they would tell me that that encounter still marked a turning point in their lives.

One of the young men was a star pupil and athlete. Though he wasn't in any of my classes, he had been coming to the bible study since a few of his friends had encountered Jesus. He'd had the "purpose in my life" encounter, and was shaking up some teachers and parents with his radical ideas. The Biology teacher was arguing with him and asked him, "How can you know this stuff is real? How can you prove it?" This happened about two weeks after he'd met Jesus.

He stood in front of the class and thought for a

moment about all of the changes he'd been experiencing in his mind and heart, and the new vision he had for his life. *"I'm* the proof that it's real!" he exclaimed with a thrill of revelation, and he walked out of the room.

It was track season, and I heard that he had begun to have blackouts during practice. His parents had taken him to doctors and they'd found a tumor on his brain. He was going up to Grand Junction to the neurologist for some final tests and diagnosis.

The day I heard about it I felt a great urge to go and pray for him. At the end of the school day I walked from the shop into the main hallway looking for him, and as I walked toward the front doors I saw him crossing the parking lot toward his car. I started to doubt and question what I'd felt, as well as wonder how weird it would be to run out after him. *"If You want me to pray for him, please make him turn around and come back into the building."* He arrived at his car and stopped. He thought a moment and looked down, then up. Then he headed straight back toward the front doors.

I met him and we went into the shop; he was completely willing and glad to be prayed for. His headache immediately left. When he went to the doctor the next day, no tumor was found! *Praise You, Jesus!*

BACKPACKING THROUGH
THE GRAND CANYON

In the summers my buddy Jody and I would take the boys on backpacking trips in the San Juan Mountains and show them the splendor of God. We'd teach them to listen and they would hear God tell them wonderful things. One year I took four boys to the Grand Canyon. A permit is required to hike into the canyon and camp there, and normally the campsites must be reserved six months to a year in advance. We picked a random date that month, wrote a request, and within a week received the most surprising reply that, yes, there was a sudden cancellation and we could have a permit for the days we had chosen. *Thank You.*

We left the farm at the start of the trip in high spirits. Five bodies and backpacks were stuffed into my Volvo station wagon along with blaring music, laughter, banter, and the constantly moving parts of four teenage boys as they wiggled, fought, expressed, and vied for space. When we got to the first mountain pass, the car died. We rolled it around and back down toward the valley, and finally it jump-started and we drove to a gas station. It was a fairly new car, the newest I'd ever owned. Nothing seemed out of order. While we were filling the tank, we laughed and caroused around the pumps, wrestled a little, and I body slammed a kid to the pavement just for fun. The boys had tons of energy. Then we brushed ourselves off, climbed into the Volvo, and headed back over the pass. This time we made it with no problems, but at the next pass it stalled again. We messed and mechanicked, but to no avail. I got an idea.

"Let's each get alone in our own space and ask God to show us what's wrong."

Now these were not all church kids, and several were not even believers yet. They looked at me with puzzlement, but they were game. One sat in the car, another walked into the woods, while two others sat down in the grass. A few minutes went by.

"Okay, what's He saying?"

Slowly they started speaking: "Well I think God is saying that we're just going off on our own adventure and we forgot to talk to Him about it."

"Yeah, like we're having this great time and not even thinking about Him."

"It's like we left Him out."

"I think He wants us to get right with Him. I don't even know what that means."

I told them about confessing, agreeing with Him, and admitting when we're wrong. We talked about repentance, changing our mind, thinking differently, and going in a different direction with it.

"Now let's do business. You guys pray out loud and tell Him what you're thinking." They were awesome. If I were God I'd have been delighted. I was moved by their pure simplicity and sincerity of heart.

Then I heard myself say: "Now we're going to all place our hands on the hood of the car, pray, and tell it to start. Then we're going to get inside and it will start and we are going to drive away. Got it?" They nodded, but with a kind of awe mixed with skepticism mixed with "This whole thing is way off my grid."

We did short business with the prayer and command and jumped in the car. All eyes and ears were tuned in to the key in the ignition. Faces lit up as the engine kicked in and we took off.

"IT WORKED!" The kids were stunned. Then we all

hooted, and I couldn't stop laughing.

We camped in the desert that night and made it to the South Rim airport the next day. A friend met us there and flew us to the North Rim in his private plane, where he dropped us off in an open meadow. From there we planned to hike for four days down into the canyon and back up the South Rim. It was completely awesome flying over the Grand Canyon in a tiny plane. It took three trips to get us and our gear all across, and it was late afternoon by the time we hiked into the campground on the North Rim. The gatekeeper said it was completely full; we had not reserved a spot on top, only down in the canyon, but it was too late to head in. We walked around the campground looking for a place to squeeze in between the others. There was one motor home with a small grassy spot by it that was unoccupied. I knocked on the door and an older gentleman told us to get off his spot, with emphasis.

I took the boys over to the edge of the rim, and we talked about blessing and not taking offense. We asked God to find us a spot and discussed His desire to be involved with us. As we explored along the rim we marveled at the beauty of the canyon, its vastness, and the shades of orange and rose highlighted in the setting sun.

A man walked up to us and asked to speak with us. His demeanor was so kind that I barely recognized him as the angry man from the campsite. With incredible humility he apologized for being so rude to us. He had followed us over to the rim and been struck by the nature of our conversation and felt he had terribly misjudged us. Would we please join him and his wife for dinner and stay at their site? Yea-ah!

The next morning after breakfast as we tightened up our packs, I asked the guys: "So, shall we have a little fun and take off by ourselves today, or shall we go with God?"

"WITH GOD!!" resounded from all of them!

The trip was phenomenal. We spent the next four days exploring pools and natural water slides, rocky cliffs, and side canyons with intricate waterfalls creating their own lush oasis environments in the middle of a sandstone desert. The contrast between the rugged beauty of the canyon and the delicate details of the plant life was astounding and delightful. We talked about the creation and the Creator, marveling at the superb design features that were carefully woven into our complex surroundings. All the boys asked to meet Jesus and keep experiencing life in His Kingdom. He delighted us the whole way and led us into amazing discoveries. I felt all I wanted to do in life was to continue to introduce young princes to the King and His Kingdom.

THE SHIRT SHRINKS

I thought my life was heavenly just living on the farm with Linda and my three kids. Linda's Grandma and my cousin Paul had joined us at this time, extending our family. I loved teaching wild boys, and I was also coaching wrestling, getting intimately involved in their victories and defeats. The Wednesday morning bible studies and the hikes and camping trips just took me deeper into their lives. I was learning a lot about what it meant to be a father, teacher, coach. I loved it.

I remember the time a couple of the boys called me up on a Tuesday night during Spring Break. "Mr. Parry, are we having bible study tomorrow morning?"

"It's Spring Break, guys! Do you want to come in at seven a.m.?"

"Yeah."

"Hey, I'll be there if you will!" Who would have thought?!

It was a small farm town where everyone knew one another. A teacher has a respected position, as does a coach. I became friends with many of the students' parents, and they were truly grateful for the love and energy I was pouring into their kids. I was finding ways to tutor kids in math, algebra, and English, set in the framework of the daily Shop experience, and watching the kids blossom. The first year I was ruthless, and for safety reasons kicked students out of my classes if they messed around. By the second year kids were begging to get into Shop class, and by the third year they were petitioning the principal for two-hour sessions. We took three students to the State Industrial Arts Fair, where they won three blue ribbons.

At the end of each year, I would write a personal note to each of my students, expressing what I saw in them and what they had meant to me. On the last day of class I would give each of them a sheet of paper and tell them to write anything they wanted to say to me and it would not affect their grade. After the students handed them in I would give each of them the note I had written. I was amazed at how honest and honoring and sensitive those bad boys were; I kept their notes for years.

I'd been teaching in Delta County for six years, but the last three years at Hotchkiss High School were my dream job; I thought I could do it forever. So in the spring of 1987 when I learned that my position was being terminated, I was dumbfounded. The official statement was that state funds were available to develop a Technology Department and Shop was being phased out, as there was a Vo-Ag program and a county-wide Vo-Tech program for those interested in shop skills. As I did not have tenure, I was being cut.

The support I received was astonishing. Teachers told me it wasn't fair. Both students and parents said they would petition the school district. When the principal was gone one day and the Band teacher was acting principal, she sent me a letter on official principal stationary stating that I was being re-hired forever at twice the pay. The graduating class even asked me to be the Baccalaureate speaker, and I got to tell a thousand people the Good News of the Kingdom of God! But there was talk that the termination had something to do with my "religious activity" at school. I needed to know how to respond to all this.

"What are You doing, Lord?"

About this time I had bought a shirt. It was a really nice-looking shirt, and I liked it a lot. I'd worn it three times and people had commented each time on how great it looked on me and how great I looked in it. Then Linda washed it. I never knew a shirt could shrink that much. I was a little bummed.

Back at school, I decided to do a Jericho March around the shop, like in the book of Joshua in the bible,

70

and make a few declarations: *"Lord, if this is You and You are taking this job, I gladly release this job and thank You for the joy these three years have brought me. Take me wherever You want. But if this is the enemy, I'm declaring that my life and livelihood and this job do not belong to him, they are the Lord's, and he cannot touch them. Back off!"* And then the Lord started to speak to me.

"Remember that shirt? How well it looked on you three times. This job is like that shirt. You've worn it for three years and it's been a great fit. People have even complimented you. But if you try to wear it another year it will be too small. I have something bigger for you." And with that came the perfect peace to move into the great unknown with Him once again.

BUILDING A CAMP BY FAITH

The spiritual community we were a part of at the time was turning a small farm on a mesa above town into "The King's Training Camp." This was a community dedicated to training people to live simply and by faith, in preparation to go to the nations to share the Good News of the Kingdom of God. Money was scarce and I was without a job, but I'd seen the faithfulness of God so often that I decided to build the kitchen of the camp entirely by faith, praying in every piece of lumber and hardware and building all the cabinets, counters, tables, and benches by hand. It was great fun, and after starting the project in the summer, our extended family celebrated Thanksgiving there with a huge feast, a large gathering of friends, and lots of joy, and I think we even had a snowball fight.

THE VILLAGE IDIOT

Being a schoolteacher in a small town is a position of respect. You get to know the parents and siblings of your students, and if you're doing a good job, you're even liked. Plus you have a salary when times are hard, when the coal mines shut down, and when the fruit trees freeze. It's a good thing. Losing my job wasn't so bad, as I had the assurance that God was leading me into something better fitting, though I had no clue what it was. I knew I was simply working for Him. And that's where it became a little hard to explain.

I'd see colleagues from the school district from time to time in town, and even parents of the students. I substitute taught, but then it was especially difficult, as people would always ask me what I was doing. Since I'd started building the camp by faith, I knew I was really working for the Lord, that it was He who was paying my way. All our needs were being met in truly miraculous ways, and we lacked for nothing. But when they asked those questions, all I could honestly say was: "I'm working for the Lord now." It sounded a little sketchy, and I had no job or realm of influence one could see in the natural, no tangible security, no position or title. It was humbling every time I said it, and the eyes would roll and the smirks would appear on faces. Old colleagues would laughingly ask: "Does He pay well? Ha, ha." Actually, yes. But it looked ridiculous. Or rather, I did. I felt like the Village Idiot in their eyes. Except that I also felt the pride and delight of my Father; I could feel His pleasure every time I answered them, so I kept on doing it.

And then one day I overheard a conversation in Heaven. I don't really know how it happened, but I heard the Father, Jesus, and the Holy Spirit talking about me. They spoke together and said to each other: "Looks like he's working for Us now. We might as well put him on salary." And that's what happened. From that time on I've never lacked wages. We started a church, really a community of spiritual adventurers, in a town of 432 people with only three families attending at first, and I never had to work at an extra job, but all our needs were covered. Then I worked for two years at an in-house drug and alcohol center that paid me $700 a month, and during that time I purchased a piece of property on the river and put a house on it, later selling it for a good profit. We took teams to Russia and Africa and started an outreach to the Rainbow Gathering where we fed thousands of people, became pastors of a tiny family of believers in a town of 2,000 and started a School of the Spirit there, and still we never lacked for money and continued to give to and feed countless people. There's no limit to the ways He's met our financial needs, but He's always been faithful and we've always gotten paid. He's good.

Chapter Four

RAISING THE DEAD

GRANDMA COMES BACK FROM DEATH

Linda's Grandma had been living with us for four years. She had adopted Linda as a baby and raised her, and when she couldn't get around by herself Linda went to Portland and brought her back to Colorado on a train. When I started teaching in the public school we moved into the old farmhouse, with running water, electricity, and a real bathroom complete with a tub and shower. It was a whole 500 square feet of living space! Linda and I slept in the living room and the three kids slept in the attic, up a ladder that leaned into the opening over the kitchen table, right next to the wood-burning cookstove. My cousin Paul slept in the tipi in the field behind the vegetable garden. And I fixed up a 1940s' Airstream-style trailer for Grandma, remodeled the interior, and pulled it up by the back porch. Then I built a smooth boardwalk out of Douglas fir tongue-and-groove floorboards I'd recycled from a house I'd torn down in the old mining town of

Bowie. The boardwalk reached from the porch to her trailer so she could get to the house with her walker. I finished it just in time to take the kids to pick her up at the train station in Grand Junction.

Grandma and the kids were wonderful together. She'd tell them stories of riding to school on a horse in the snow with her sister Lily and growing up in Calgary, Alberta, with six siblings. They entertained her with their antics and stories, and they all got their love tanks filled daily. And she stopped reading dark crime novels and started reading the bible and historical fiction. But most exciting was when her talk of the "little baptism" (sprinkling) and the old Lutheran church services she used to attend that were conducted in high German changed to talk of her desire to meet Jesus Christ and have the "big baptism" (immersion). Her baptism took place outside in a horse trough filled with fresh water when she was 83!

When we moved to the camp on Hanson Mesa, we moved Grandma's trailer and boardwalk with us. She got sick that winter and Linda took her to a doctor, who said her heart was slowing down. Linda and I both had the feeling that Grandma was dying, but we never put it into words.

I was working on the barn with a friend one day, and I went inside to make lunch for Grandma and myself. We were talking as I heated up some soup, when all of a sudden Grandma made a strange gurgling noise and started to fall over on the couch. I leaped over to her and caught her as she was going down. I ended up sitting on the couch with Grandma's shoulders and head in my lap, and she just stopped. Stopped everything: breathing, moving, looking, talking, smiling, being warm. She went

76

from being warm and kind of limp to cold and stiff, and from pinkish to grey. I just held her and felt an amazing holy awe. I was thinking how she and all of our kids had been born at home, and how natural it was to die at home. There was a real sweetness to it. She was 84 and had lived a full life, but lately she had been sick more often, felt weaker, and had a much harder time getting around. She'd met Jesus and was ready to go.

But then my mind started exploring strange new options. I'd never had anyone die in my lap before. Do you call 911? Does the ambulance come with the paramedics to jump start her and then leave her in a bed all hooked up for the next months or years? Do the cops come with their lights flashing outside and walk around in your holy space and ask questions and take notes? Just what does one do? I was really treasuring the holy awe, and was just asking the Lord what to do, when I thought about Linda and the kids.

Linda had driven down to town with the kids a couple of hours before and was not reachable by phone. I thought about how Grandma had raised her when she had been rejected by her own mother, and that she would be grieved not to have been there to say goodbye. And the kids would need to say goodbye as well.

"What should I do, Lord?"

"Rebuke death," came the answer almost instantly. Okay. So I did.

Immediately I saw a grey-black cloud that lifted up off Grandma and flew out through the wall of the trailer. I looked at her, and soon after that I heard a sound, very faint, from deep, deep within her. A tiny breath was being activated somewhere deep inside her and I could hear it. When I heard it I began to pray and with increasing emphasis and energy and enthusiasm commanded life to come into her. I was speaking fast and breathing hard and I began to hear a sucking, breathing sound that increased as it continued. Color was coming into her face and the stiffness and cold were leaving. I prayed faster. I was getting excited! Her eyes fluttered and opened! I looked into her face and eyes and called her name: "Emma!" We connected.

"Grandma, are you ready to go and be with Jesus forever?"

She looked around her as if to check on her surroundings. Then she told me, "Yes." As she looked around she asserted that she definitely did not want to stay here if it meant lying around and being bedridden!

Just then my friend Elden, who was working on the barn, came in.

"Quick, go down to town and find Linda and tell her to come up here really fast!"

He saw Grandma, still in my arms, and rushed out the door. Now she was ready to sit up, and I sat her beside me and we talked. By the time Linda arrived we were laughing and carrying on like nothing had happened. But when I saw Linda and the kids, I said: "Give Grandma a big hug and a kiss and tell her you love her!"

The kids all gathered around her and loved her. Linda looked quizzically at me and I explained what had happened. So Linda got out her blood-pressure cuff and began to check Grandma out.

Things seemed back to normal, so I was getting ready to go back out to the barn when Linda told me that things were *not* okay.

"Grandma doesn't have *any* blood pressure!" Linda exclaimed. Oh boy.

We gathered around her and just visited and talked. After a while Jesse went out to play, and Faith, who was having a hard time with the thought that Grandma might leave us again, went into the house to avoid seeing it happen. Linda and Grace and I spent the afternoon in the trailer with Grandma. She was sitting on the couch holding Grace's hand and we were talking, and all of a sudden I heard a sound and turned toward her and she lurched forward and a death rattle came out of her throat. We laid her out on the couch and stayed there in that holy space. We eventually called Faith and Jesse in, and all of us spent about an hour praying and singing and talking.

Now I was left with my original predicament: what do you do with a dead person? *After* you've already raised her from the dead and now it's time to release her; she's 84 and she definitely does not want to come back. Linda was hesitant to have anyone come in too quickly, and felt like she needed time to let go. We waited a long while, and I finally called dispatch for the coroner, who told me he'd send over an officer from the sheriff's department. I prayed for favor, and the most curious thing happened. The only officer I personally knew was a man in whose house we had held a bible study a while ago. He'd only recently become a Christian, and had even met Grandma on several occasions. And he's the one they sent! He was extremely loving and non-invasive. He gave us plenty of time and even prayed with us as he filled out his report in a completely non-threatening way. It was still hard to release Grandma's body to the coroner, but he had been waiting patiently outside all this time, so we finally called him in and he assured Linda she could spend more time with her at the mortuary if she wanted.

God was so amazingly good to us to give Linda that time to say goodbye and connect one last time with the woman who had chosen her and adopted her and raised her. And He showed us that His compassion toward us is greater than death

SPYING OUT THE LAND

We were meeting with a hundred or so people in a little building in Hotchkiss, seeing God transform lives, heal people, and fill them with the Holy Spirit. I was still knocking on doors to talk to people about the goodness of God, when we devised a plan to take teams of our people and to cover all the towns in Western Colorado. I headed up a team of three and we went through the southern part of the region, going through ten towns in four different rural counties. I'd already covered six towns in Delta County the previous two years. At the time I wasn't completely sure what the assignment actually was in doing this, but I was growing in freedom and boldness, and I felt a promise had been highlighted to me from the book of Joshua in the bible, in the first chapter, where God told Joshua to go over to the land *He was giving him:*

> *"Every place that the sole of your foot will tread upon*
> *I have given you ... be strong and of good courage;*
> *do not be afraid, nor be dismayed,*
> *for the Lord your God is with you wherever you go."*

On one of these journeys the three of us camped out in the mountain town of Ouray, which really means we slept in the grass somewhere, and on Sunday morning my two companions and I prayed: "Lord, please lead us to a church that is having a pot-luck dinner so we can eat lunch!" I'm sure we prayed something about meeting people who were hungry for God and about having the opportunity to get to know some folks in a more relational way than just being in a church meeting. But I remember the lunch part because when we arrived at the church they announced that everyone was invited up to one family's mountain cabin for a barbecue after the meeting. It doesn't get much better than that. And that's where we met our hosts, Tim and Paula, who were to become some of our closest friends over the next 20 years.

The folks from that little church asked us on several occasions if we would send someone up to preach and teach in their mountain town, and I went a few times, as did some of our other men. A couple of their families from Ouray County also came to our meetings in Hotchkiss once or twice, and they eventually asked if we would send someone to establish a fellowship of believers who wanted to be led by and experience more of the Holy Spirit. They lived in Ridgway, a town of about 430 people nestled in a valley at the entrance to the San Juan Mountains.

We all prayed about it, and the pastor of our group in Hotchkiss called a meeting one Saturday night. Basically the Holy Spirit said, "Now separate to Me Chuck and Linda for the work to which I have called them." All the men laid hands on me and prayed over me as they commissioned me to go. But Linda and I still needed to know for ourselves. She was ready to go if we got the word, so I told her I was going to spend some time upstairs in the barn until I heard from God. I walked through the same kitchen I had built by faith a year and a half before in the old barn, and then climbed the stairs to a room we'd made into a library and prayer room. I'd built the bookshelves, which covered the west wall and were now about half full. Everything was familiar; I'd had a long-term dream of being part of a teaching and training facility that prepared people to walk in the power of the Holy Spirit to bring the life of the Kingdom of God into all the realms of this world. Yet I felt that this wasn't that dream. I began to praise and worship God. Almost instantly I felt the rush of His Presence as He spoke a scripture right into my heart, and I knew we were supposed to go:

"How beautiful upon the mountains are the feet of him
who brings good news, who proclaims peace,
who brings glad tidings of good things,
who proclaims salvation, who says to Zion,
'Your God reigns!'
Listen! Your watchmen shall lift up their voices,
with their voices they shall sing together;
for they shall see with their own eyes
when the Lord restores Zion."
Isaiah 52:7, 8

I went back into our house and told Linda I'd heard. She was startled, as she thought I'd be gone for half the day. Not so this time.

We started meeting in the Ridgway Town Hall in the spring of 1989. After 16 years in the North Fork Valley, the Lord was leading us into a new land in the San Juan

Mountains, among new people. We didn't know then that we would stay in that region for the next 20 years.

The only rule we made for our meetings was that we would not limit our time in worship or in receiving what the Holy Spirit wanted to do in our midst. Linda and I loved being in the Presence of God and wanted to experience more time in that awesome Presence with a group of people to see where He would take us. There's the Presence of God that is always there, but then there's the *Manifest Presence*, when a group of people can corporately feel and respond to the recognizable Presence of God moving in their midst. I wanted the freedom to explore that without limitations and to take a group of hungry adventurers on a journey into realms of possibility (and impossibility) that we had never explored before.

It took a little while to get going, as we needed to sow some new ideas into the realm of Sunday Morning Meetings as people knew them. The group's familiarity with the common church service and traditions, together with the level of comfort and preferences of each individual, was working against our having a real and supernatural encounter with God. I know that God can move within the confines of these things, but I was hungry for a corporate experience that was out of the normal box. I remember telling a friend before we moved to Ridgway that I was willing to do this experiment only if it was going to be a Work of God. He countered with: "What if God wants you to go and just start a regular, normal church?" "Then I think I'm the wrong guy for the job," I responded.

Our vision was to have an intimate spiritual community of closely-knit people who wanted more of God and less of religion and form. At first we suffered severe opposition, both from our sending church and from one of the families in our new community, but as we pressed in closer to the Holy Spirit things began to dramatically change. We also began to attract "all that were discontented and in distress and in debt," just like David in the bible had done when he fled from King Saul and hid out in a cave in the wilderness in First Samuel chapter 22. God spoke to me that He wanted to change those distressed ones into "David's Mighty Men," just as He had back then, if we'd work with Him. We started having everyone over for lunch at our house after the meetings, as we were especially interested in building relationships and family. On the holidays we had sit-down dinners in our home for more than 60 people. At our first Christmas dinner in Ridgway, an older couple from the church gave me a gift. The woman had bought a hand-painted work of calligraphy on which Isaiah 52:7-8 was beautifully written out and colored, looking like a page from an ancient manuscript. She'd had it for years, not knowing who was supposed to receive it. Her husband had framed it in barn wood salvaged from the ruins of an old ghost town in the mountains above us, and they presented it to me, not having any idea that it was the same scripture verse God had spoken to me when I'd sought His will in the barn nine months before. It was a wonderful encouragement.

We pastored the church in Ridgway for six years, and it grew into a community of spiritual adventurers who took on challenges, loved risk, and went into the parks, the jails, each other's hearts and homes, and into the nations with the love of God. That little church of around 100 people sent some of our mighty ones to Europe, Africa, South America, and Asia. People came from five different counties, driving for up to two hours to join us for our Sunday celebrations. These meetings could last from two to four hours and were not for the faint of heart. We didn't have any "bench warmers," as only those came who really wanted what was happening in our midst. During the week, we held meetings in homes in the different communities that were represented. It was a beautiful fellowship of individuals I still consider some of my favorite friends. As I look back at that time, I see that people were drawn to that fellowship of believers from all of the towns through which I had walked and knocked on doors. Later, when I became the pastor up in Telluride, several of us started a monthly meeting called "Seeking God for a Move of His Spirit." For three years we met in various towns, and we began to notice that everyone who was drawn to our meetings desired to see God's supernatural gifts being manifested in the midst of His people. They were all seeking "revival," whatever that might be, and many of them felt called to pray for churches and believers in Western Colorado to see "revival" break out there. We called them "intercessors."

One night when I was driving from Grand Junction, at the northern end of the Western Slope of Colorado, to Telluride, the southern mountain gate to our Western Slope, I had a vision. There's a big stretch of desert to drive through and the road was dark and the sky exploded with millions of stars. Suddenly I was taken up to where I could see the whole Western Slope, and in each of its towns I saw bright lights shining. The Lord told me that the bright lights were believers in each town, and that He wanted us to begin to gather together praying people from each community who would connect with one another. He wanted these people to network together to pray for a common goal of revival for all of His church in Western Colorado. We spent the next few years connecting prayer warriors and seeing a network begin to develop, where people knew one another and came together to see God's move increase in our midst. I saw again that God was drawing hungry people from all of the towns He'd had me walk through. I was only a small facilitator, but He has a great plan for these folks He loves who live in the mountains, mesas, and valleys of Western Colorado.

COUNTY JAIL

My first visit to the Delta County Jail came as the result of a tragedy. Friends of ours had a young son around the age of our Jesse, who was about three years old. The boys had played together, and it was a terrible shock when our friends called to tell us their son had been run over by a drunk driver. We rushed down to comfort them and grieve with them. We didn't get to see the child's body to pray for life to come into it, but we saw a different kind of resurrection.

Apparently the young driver had just had a break-up with his wife and was very distraught. Alcohol, depression, the late afternoon sun's brightness, and a small boy on a bike became the ingredients for tragedy. Though our friends grieved for their son, they felt a greater grief for the young man who had no hope. They asked if I would visit him in the jail and tell him they forgave him.

He was deep in torment and felt he had committed the unforgivable and unpardonable sin in taking an innocent child's life. The message I shared with him of

God's forgiveness and how He gave the life of His innocent and blameless Son in exchange for our guilt and shame was new to him. He understood sin and judgment, punishment and wrath, but not mercy, grace, or forgiveness. At first he couldn't receive it. I asked if he would be willing to study the bible with me over the next months and he accepted the offer. Soon he met Jesus himself and he suddenly had hope, his life was turned around, and I got addicted to visiting the county jail! I'd check the roster each week to see who was in jail that I knew and ask if they wanted a visit. During the next 25 years I held bible studies and prayed with inmates in jails and a state prison in five counties.

There was a time when so many of those men were experiencing God's power and love that the very atmosphere of the jail was changing. Men were being filled with great joy and finding an immense peace that surpassed all understanding, especially considering their circumstances. We were having outrageous celebrations, and the men were seeing into a different Kingdom, glimpsing a whole new way of life. The law-enforcement officers were especially noticing the transformation. I actually asked the undersheriff if I could be admitted and stay in the cells for a week or two to disciple the men and establish them in the Truth before they were sent off to prison. I wanted time to encourage and teach the new believers so they could experience the Presence of God more strongly. The undersheriff told me I was nuts, and then told me absolutely NO, specifically for insurance reasons. But he continued to notice the transformation and gave me great favor.

I developed good relationships with undersheriffs

and officers in several counties, but one of them became special to me. I'll call him Mr. Read. He was a rough and coarse, western kind of guy and definitely not a Christian. But he had a good sense of humor and humored me in my mischief. I had quite a few entertaining conversations with him. On one occasion he was telling me how he went to church one time, and I responded with: "Undersheriff Read, going to church doesn't make you a Christian any more than going into a donut shop makes you a cop." I think he called donuts "crime-fighting biscuits." He was ornery and he joked with me a lot, but I could tell he really cared about the condition of his jail, and the inmates were truly benefiting from that. I began to pray for him.

One day I asked if I could speak with him after I was finished with the men and our celebration. He ushered me down the hall into his office, sat down behind his desk, and offered me the chair facing him. I held up my bible and said:

"Did you know that it speaks about you in this book?"

He stood up, extended his hand to shake mine, and replied: "Mr. Parry, it's been nice talking to you," indicating that our conversation was terminated.

"No, really. It says in here that you are God's minister of good for those who do good, and of correction for those who do evil. You're God's man, and you have authority from Him to keep order and peace. So I just wanted to tell you that I'm praying for you for your success — that you will be able to do a great job with excellence and accomplishment. I'm praying for you to succeed at all that you put your hands to, for your ideas and strategies to bear fruit, and your jail to be the very best it can be while you serve here."

He was stunned. He looked away, and I saw that his eyes were getting a little wet. "No one's ever said that to me before. Thank you." He seemed really uncomfortable, so I shook his hand and made my exit, and I continued to pray for him.

A week later he asked if I'd come into his office when I was finished in the jail. I was curious. He offered me a cup of coffee and told me about a plan he had that he needed help with. He had been rounding up old bicycles and tools and wanted to have the inmates fix up the bikes for poor kids in town for Christmas. This would give the men something to do as well as allow them to be useful to the community. I liked it! He told me that unfortunately the county and the sheriff's department weren't behind it and no money could be found to help implement the plan. I gave him $500 from our church's benevolent fund, and he was overwhelmed. He kept me posted on the progress; it was a great success in the eyes of those kids who received the bikes, and he actually received a little positive feedback for his efforts.

The river of life flowing into the jail increased, and I was allowed to bring in friends with guitars to lead worship. We put together a team from our church and made up dramas and skits to present on holidays, like the Fourth of July and Thanksgiving. These skits would generally draw a larger crowd, and we were eventually allowed to meet with the women as well. The men and women from our community of believers poured their hearts into the inmates, giving up their own holidays to be with them, and then staying in touch with them through their prison sentences and helping them when they got out of jail. I saw those who had been "discontented and in distress and in debt" become givers and lovers and teachers. I saw people growing on both sides, and it gave me immense pleasure!

Then at about two o'clock one morning, the phone rang. Grace answered it, and as I came out of my bedroom she held her hand over the receiver and whispered to me that there was a man asking for me, and he sounded strange. I took the phone.

"Hello, this is Chuck."

"Mr. Parry, I have the barrel of a shotgun aimed at the inside of my mouth, and I want to know if you can give me one good reason why I shouldn't pull the trigger."

"Well, you just called me, so that's reason enough. You're important to me." I started praying in tongues and talking really fast, keeping the conversation going in a meaningful way. I didn't ask him how he was feeling, but I affirmed him in all the ways he was awesome and remarkable. When he became more rational and calm, I could tell he was working hard not to cry. Something about the conversation was touching his emotions. He began to tell me about the impact I had made on his life.

"Undersheriff Read, can I meet you for breakfast in a few hours? Will you promise you won't shoot yourself tonight?" He promised. "Do you think you're likely to get any sleep?" He said he was tired, and I felt safe in saying goodbye, certain that I would see him in the morning.

The next day he told me about all the pain and betrayal and disappointment in his life. He was divorced

90

from his wife, estranged from his grown sons, and going to lose his job. He was around 55, and it looked to him as if his whole life had added up to zero. So I told him about God's love, about Jesus, and about the love God put in my heart toward him. I looked at him and all I could do was love him. He kept breaking down in tears and having to walk out of the room, but I assured him that in this Kingdom where I lived it was really okay to cry. I shared some astounding things about God's love and His Kingdom with Mr. Read, and I asked if I could get together with him once a week, or even more often, to study the bible with him. He was willing. Every time we got together he cried. It was very uncomfortable for him, but I saw things begin to change in his tough demeanor and new hope begin to creep in. When his job actually ended, he began to look at it as the beginning of a new adventure rather than the end of a failed life. He traveled a bit and then moved away, but he would come back and visit Linda and me whenever he was in the area. He liked to hunt, and one day he offered to lend me a beautiful, older Winchester 30.06 rifle to go hunting. The next time he came around I tried to return it, but he refused to take it back. Now it was a gift from a friend, in gratitude for saving his life. I look at it fondly as a trophy of God's goodness toward the hopeless and hurting. He just changes lives, and I have 25 years of memories of those in jail who have met Him and have never been the same again. County jail is a good fishing hole, a great place for the river to flow in, fill up, overflow out, and take many lives and families into a new Kingdom where love rules and there's a new King who changes all the rules and transforms lives.

CRACK-HOUSE DRUNK

I'd been studying the bible with a young man in the county jail who had begun to experience God in powerful ways. He asked if he could be baptized, and we were given permission to do so in the Intake Room shower one afternoon right there in the jailhouse. The young man continued to do well as long as he was in jail, but each time he got out he would return to his old friends and go back to using drugs.

One Sunday morning eight of us were praying together at the church when a woman burst in and announced that this same young man, whom I'll call Clyde in this story, had apparently drunk some toxic poison, some kind of flammable fuel, and he thought he was dying. A few people rushed out to find him, but I was sure I wasn't supposed to go, so the rest of us stayed behind and prayed for him and then continued to gather with many others, play music, and praise and worship God. As I checked in with the Holy Spirit, I was confident that we were doing the thing that gave God pleasure.

Around three o'clock in the afternoon I was alone and headed over to the place where I knew Clyde had been staying. It was a room on the second floor above a Cajun restaurant on one of the side streets in town. Several people I'd known who used drugs heavily had stayed there at different times, as the rent was cheap. I'd actually never been in the room, but I knew it was in the back corner because people had called out to me from the window as I'd walked down the alley on numerous occasions. So I climbed the dark stairway to the second floor hall and explored. Finding the door, I knocked loudly and heard a moan from inside, and Clyde's voice croaked: "Come in."

The room was twilit, as there was an old bed sheet hanging over the window. A mattress lay on the floor against the wall, and Clyde lay groaning on the mattress. Though I asked him, it was difficult for me to comprehend from what he was saying what the fuel was and how and why he had drunk it, but I clearly understood that he was in intense pain. He said he had gone to the clinic and that he couldn't eat or sleep, and that he had been tossing about on the old mattress for several days, unable to find rest or peace.

"Can I pray for you?"

"Yeah, I need it." I placed my hand on his belly and he began to lie still and relax. Peace came over him and he started to doze off, and then he apologized, but his eyelids closed and he lay completely still, breathed deeply and slowly, and then fell asleep. I was sure he was fine, as he lay there sound asleep.

A deep and pervasive peace filled the entire room, wrapping me up in it like a rich blanket. The Presence of God was thick in the place. I basked in it. Then I looked around at the carpet on which I was sitting cross-legged and at the debris that lay scattered throughout the room. Assorted paraphernalia was embedded in the semi-shag rug and there was a dingy smell and feel to the room, so I decided I didn't need to remain any longer. But then I tried to get up. I felt like I was drunk! I could barely move and was completely off balance. I lunged for the door and leaned against it with my hand on the knob. I started laughing and turned, with my back against the door, almost sliding down the face of it to the floor. I couldn't stop laughing!

I'd been "drunk in the Holy Spirit" before, but always with a group of people, never alone. And never in a crack house! I made it out the door and managed to close it, then reeled across the hall to grab the stair rail. I was still laughing. A couple came up the stairs and laughed as they passed me in the dim light, while I just stood there holding on to the railing trying not to lose it completely. *"I need to get out of here."*

Down the stairs and out into the sunlight I kept moving, but the ridiculous feeling of euphoria wouldn't leave me. As I staggered up the incline of the street, I remember thinking that no matter how foolish I might look, I liked this! The next challenge was to turn the corner onto Main Street. Two long blocks to go until I could turn up my street and find a hiding place where I could be completely wrecked in privacy.

I moved slowly up Main Street, leaning against the buildings with my hands and walking with them along the brick and glass storefronts on the south side of the street. Sitting across the street at the tables in front of the coffee shop, the Sunday afternoon crowd sipping cappuccinos and lattés suddenly caught sight of me. They hailed me with laughter and joking, wondering what I was up to. I sort of waved back and chuckled to myself.

"God, You are so funny. This is so funny. I don't care what I look like or what anyone says. If I can feel like this, this good, I don't care if I look ridiculous. And if You're going to heal someone when I pray for them, You can get me drunk anytime. This is so funny." I remember thinking for a second about my reputation, but that *really* made me laugh, and I thought: *"Drunk people just don't care!"*

94

I made it to safety and lay on the floor, on my own carpet, for several hours, laughing and rejoicing in the goodness of God. Clyde later told me that he slept until the next morning, woke up ravenous, and went out and ate a big breakfast. Clyde got healed and I got drunk in the Holy Ghost; now that was a good afternoon!

REBUKING DEATH IN UGANDA

In January of 1995, Linda and I took a team of ten, including our youngest two children, to Uganda for a month. There are many miraculous stories to tell from that trip, but this one particularly stands out. We were in a village working with a pastor and his wife, and before we caught the *matatu* (a 14-passenger Toyota van that operated as public transportation) back to the city where we had rented a house above Lake Victoria, he asked if we would go with him to pray for a "sick woman." I took four others and we walked to the woman's hut.

As we entered the hut, we were overwhelmed by the stench of death and decay, defecation, and rotting flesh. I almost gagged at the smell in the warm, tropical air. On the floor there was a sheet of black plastic upon which lay a naked black woman. She was reduced to skin and bones and her skin was an ashen grey hue. Her eyes remained wide open and bulging but the whites were brownish-yellow in color. A thin black plastic garbage bag was spread over her torso for a covering. It was a bit more than I'd had in mind when I thought of a "sick woman." *"Is she alive or dead?"*

The five of us formed a circle around her body and began to worship God. The air seemed to clear up a little, and we prayed and sang until we felt a strong sense of His Presence. And then we simply rebuked death. As we did, a black cloud suddenly appeared on her body, rose up off her, and went up and out through the thatched roof. We began to praise God more loudly and enthusiastically, and quickly the air inside the hut began to change. The smell of death faded and was replaced with a sweet aroma, like *roses!* Her color turned from ashen grey to a rich brownish-black. And something happened to her eyes. They became *alive.* Everything about the place was becoming transformed, when a boy burst into the hut and exclaimed that the *matatu* had arrived and we had to hurry if we were to catch the last ride out of the village. We wanted to stay and see what would happen next, but we were rushed outside and up to the store by the main road where we were packed with others like sardines into the *matatu.* A week later the pastor came to visit us at our home, and we asked him what had become of the woman. "Oh, she got better," he replied. I think he's the king of understatement. But Jesus is King over life and death.

BABY COMES BACK TO LIFE OVER SKYPE

It delights me to think that God can use technology such as the internet to display His victory over life and death, and His lordship over all created things. I was on a Skype call in 2009 with a couple in the United Kingdom, and they were distraught over the woman's pregnancy. The eight-month-old baby in her womb had not moved in over a week, and they had been to the doctor for an ultrasound. They could find no heartbeat or vital signs and could not hear, feel, or see any signs of life. The doctors wanted to remove the dead baby. The parents were shocked, scared, and grieved, but they still had hope and asked me to pray.

I could see their faces on the computer screen, filled with expectation. I saw the wife's big belly and asked the husband to place his hands over it. Then all together we declared LIFE to the baby. The mother gasped and began to cry out as the baby kicked in her womb for the first time in over a week. They both began to shout and cry and jump around ecstatically as the baby continued to move and react. I have their digitalizing, joy-filled faces embedded in my memory every time I recall the event. God brought them the triumph of Jesus' victory over death and filled their home with *fullness of joy!*

Chapter Five

REVIVAL IN RUSSIA
1991~1995

ALWAYS TRIUMPHANT

In the third year after we moved to Ridgway, *LIFE* started to break out among us and people were being drawn into the community of believers from the surrounding counties in increasing numbers. They were hungry for more than "going to church," and we began to "do life together" in much deeper and more personally interactive ways. I watched those wounded ones, the ones who were "discontented, in distress, and in debt," as they spread their wings and began to look out for the needs of others. I listened as they spoke words of wisdom and courage into the hearts of the fearful. They were amazing! A pastor from Montrose, a city half an hour to the north of us, called us *"the Radically Alive Church."* I felt honored.

Then I started looking out toward the whole world.

"I want to see people grow everywhere, Lord!" About this time a crazy evangelist friend came through Ridgway and told me: "The Iron Curtain just fell! Let's go to Russia and give away bibles!" And everything inside me exploded. For years I had read stories of the underground church in Communist countries and had supported several bible-smuggling groups. One year while I was still on the farm, I became part of a project that mailed very thin pages from the gospel of John to everyone in the Leningrad phone book. I mailed a tissue-like portion of several chapters to dozens of people in airmail-letter envelopes, while others from many free countries mailed the other parts, until each address had been sent one of the complete gospels in Russian. I had been reading about smugglers and martyrs, so I was stirred when I met a man returning from Eastern Europe who told me this story:

"I arrived at the contact's home with the bibles, and he told me there would be a large meeting of believers the next day. So early in the morning we caught a bus heading out of the city. We got off out in the country, and then we walked quite a distance. We crossed some fields and entered a large forest. As we came to a clearing in the forest, we noticed people streaming in from many directions. There were many hundreds of them. 'This is an unbelievable gathering! How do you get the word out to so many people?' I asked. My guide looked puzzled. 'Oh, but we don't. It is the Holy Spirit who tells them.' No phone calls, letters, or couriers. That would be too dangerous. And after a superb time of worship in song and prayer, and much enthusiastic preaching of the word, I asked: 'This is wonderful, but it is summertime. What do you do in the winter?' Again, a puzzled look: 'Oh, but we wear our overcoats.'"

This was the culture I longed to see. My evangelist friend Rick and his wife Gerry and I obtained visas and booked flights, not knowing a soul in Moscow, not having a single connection, and not knowing a word of the language. And then the excitement began. A friend drove me six hours to Denver to catch my flight and we stayed overnight with friends of a friend who lived there. As we were visiting that night, a man who had just returned from a week in Moscow happened to stop by to see our hosts. When I told him we were going to Moscow and we knew no one there, he gave me the phone numbers of two Bulgarian university students, Dima and Dima, who had just become Christians and spoke Bulgarian, Russian, and English. (When we met, I fell in love with them, and our lives continued to intertwine for the next five years!) I went to bed on a mat on the floor, thanking and praising God for His goodness and the Divine connection. And He spoke a scripture verse to me in the night, which I memorized. I found it in Second Corinthians chapter 2:

"Thanks be to God, who always leads us in triumph in Christ Jesus, and makes manifest through us the sweet aroma of the knowledge of God everywhere we go!"

I didn't know I would be needing it the next morning.

I met Rick and Gerry at the airport in Denver. Rick had a friend who was a travel agent who had secured the tickets, as there was no searching the internet for deals in those days. He gave me my tickets and we flew to JFK Airport in New York City, where we were to board a flight to Helsinki, Finland, and from there to Moscow. This was years before there were e-tickets or airline security. We got to the gate with paper tickets just 45

101

minutes before flight time to find that my tickets from the travel agent contained the ticket from Denver to New York, and one from Helsinki to Moscow, but none from New York to Helsinki. There was, however, a return ticket from Helsinki to New York.

"I'm sorry, sir, but we have no record of your reservation to Helsinki."

"I beg your pardon?"

The woman repeated her statement and explained my predicament.

"Thanks be to God, who always leads us in triumph in Christ Jesus."

"I beg your pardon, sir?"

"Thanks be to God, who always leads us in triumph in Christ Jesus." I smiled and showed her that I had a return ticket from Helsinki to New York. She called her manager. The clock ticked away and boarding time approached. The manager arrived and asked what the problem was, which the woman explained, and then the manager explained the problem again to me.

"Thanks be to God, who always leads us in triumph in Christ Jesus." I smiled at him. I felt the Presence of God very close.

"I'll see what I can do for you, sir."

"Thanks be to God, who always leads us in triumph in Christ Jesus."

Boarding began. After some consultations and some time on the computer, he disappeared for a few minutes and then reappeared and printed out a ticket and presented it to me. "Have a nice flight, sir."

"Thanks be to God, who always leads us in triumph in Christ Jesus." I smiled at both of them and blessed them. As I walked up the corridor, I looked back and saw them talking to each other with puzzled looks on their faces. "Thanks be to God, who always leads us in triumph in Christ Jesus, and makes manifest the sweet aroma of the knowledge of God everywhere we go."

On the flight I sat next to a Mormon gentleman who told me extensively how great and large his organization was, how well organized and financially well supplied. He was going to do a great work and was well supported by his vast organization. Then he asked me what I was doing. How large was my extended church organization? What? A small church of 50 to 100? *What is it* I was doing?

The spirit of intimidation and the fear of man were beginning to weigh on me, along with the simple apprehension of seeming just plain foolish, or maybe even stupid. But I felt His Presence as strongly as ever, so I told the man about my King, how good and pure and magnificent He is; and about His Kingdom, how vast and perfect and invisible it seems, until you need it and believe, and watch it work; and how all the power of the Kingdom of God and all of creation is with me. He raised his eyebrows, smiled, and went back to reading his magazine. I became overwhelmed by the Presence and leaned back and smiled until I was glowing, and then chuckles turned to quiet laughter and I praised God for hours.

DIVINE CONNECTIONS

Arriving in Moscow was a unique experience. We could still feel the atmosphere of 70 years of oppression hanging heavily over the country, like the heaviness of the hefty, dark steel-pipe pieces welded together into a massive sculpture and hanging so that it completely covered the ceilings in the airport. Art with a message: *Heaviness*. And there were teenagers who prowled the airport corridors wearing camo and carrying automatic weapons. We had to go through some sort of government tourist-visa protocol, and found ourselves in a crowded office where the officials sounded like they were yelling at one another in Russian. We were directed to an English-speaking woman named Ludmilla, who set us up with a hotel and checked our security status. She spoke kindly, in a way that was uncommon and very comforting. I asked her if she were a Christian.

"No. I would like to be, but I sin."

"I've got great news for you ..." and I told her about the Great Exchange of her sin for God's sinlessness. Almost too good to be true. She opened up and I introduced her to Jesus.

"Thanks be to God, who always leads us in triumph in Christ Jesus, and makes manifest the sweet aroma of the knowledge of God everywhere we go."

She officially asked our purpose in Russia, and we told her we wanted to buy thousands of bibles and give them away everywhere we went. But we didn't know where we could buy them. She told us she would check into it. That was one of our only experiences with communicating in English for the next few days.

The lineup of cab drivers shouting at us in Russian and pulling at our luggage, and the general run-down appearance of the airport lobby added to the feeling that we were completely out of our element. One taxi driver attracted us with his lit-up friendly face and his remarkable ability to communicate through pantomime. His name was Victor and we hit it off right away. We stepped out into the freezing December Russian winter night and drove through almost empty streets. None of the cars had headlights on, and there were abandoned vehicles all along the route. It was eerie and kind of post-Armageddon. I remember being constantly surprised that this world super power was a third-world country. Victor found our hotel and gave us his phone number for future reference. We went to our rooms and thanked God for meeting all of our needs and opening more doors for us. I felt as if I had been in the open door of a cargo plane at 10,000 feet, and a voice had said "Jump," and I had jumped. Here I was, free-falling through time and distance with nothing under control, only the sure but irrational hope that a 'chute would open. And it did.

Ludmilla phoned in the morning and told us that the Russian Baptist Church was printing the New Covenant on the former Soviet printing presses and charging the equivalent of 11 cents apiece for them. *"Thanks be to God ...."*

It just so happened that there had been an overnight financial collapse in the economy and the ruble had dropped in value from 40 rubles to the dollar to 1,200 rubles to the dollar. Overnight. Great for our exchange rate; terrible for their economy. All the banks were closed, and we asked a young man to interpret the sign on one of them. He told us it said something like: *"Closed for technical difficulties."* He was right.

We called Victor and he waved us into the cab and took us through the city to several closed banks, finally finding possibly the only one open in Moscow. As I started to get out, he grabbed my arm to stop me and, pointing to my pack, dramatized dumping everything in my backpack onto the floor of the cab and then taking the pack inside. I didn't realize what $1,000 would look like in wads of small bills. I felt like I had robbed the bank, as the manager counted and bundled and stacked the bills and then helped me fill my pack with them. Then we toured the city, and after the three of us ate a five-course supper in a palace ballroom for a total of $20 we walked through Red Square at midnight, giddy on life. I bartered for a Russian fur hat under a streetlight, and we walked through some pretty seedy areas along with a motley assortment of late-night Russians; we talked to anyone who knew English, and tried to talk to anyone who didn't. All with about a million rubles bulging in my backpack. *"Thanks be to God ..."*

The next day we bought bibles and carted them all in boxes through the narrow hotel lobby, up the rickety and lurching 1940s' elevator, and piled them into huge stacks that filled our rooms, which were both two-room suites. Each day we packed as many boxes of bibles as we could carry onto little folding hand-carts or into the cab, and took them to different places to distribute them. Remarkable and delightful things happened.

Victor took us to Vladimir, an ancient city surrounded by an earthen mound for a defense wall. It was 14 below zero. We arrived at a Russian Orthodox cathedral built in 1157 just as the bells were ringing and the service was letting out. Flocks of *babushkas*, Russian grandmothers bundled up and wearing head scarves tied under their chins, emerged from the church. We offered each one a bible: "Biblia ... podarak ... besplatno ..." Bible, a gift, free of charge .... They held them to their breasts, cried, kissed us up and down our faces, and blessed our children's children. It was memorable. I thought about their generation being possibly the last to have seen, held, and read the bible in freedom. Everywhere we went we experienced the same reaction. Seventy years without the bible had created both hunger and curiosity.

We went to street corners, churches, Red Square, Moscow University, a children's hospital, train stations, anywhere we could find a crowd, though mostly we generated the crowds. What we found was that we really wanted to *communicate* with the people as well as bless them with bibles. So we called Dima and Dima. They had met Jesus in a rally in the stadium that summer and were crazy about Him. So they had decided to quit their studies at the university and study Jesus instead. They loved the idea of going around with some crazy Americans and telling people about His Love. I fell in love with them too, so we went all over the city together.

I remember one particular night on Red Square. Nighttime starts at about three o'clock in the afternoon in the winter there, and the Russian young people party until around two in the morning. As we entered Red Square, we noticed there was a long barricade that stretched all the way across the middle of the square, with only a small opening in the center. It funneled everyone crossing the square through that single gate. Let's set up there! We piled our cartons of bibles by the gate and gave them away to all, creating quite a bottleneck in the traffic flow. We handed out bibles and declared the goodness and love of God, with the Dimas assisting and interpreting. It got a little wild, and I had lost sight of my Dima for a while, when he came up to me and said a man wished to speak to me. I approached a distinguished looking gentleman in his fifties who stood tall in his long black dress overcoat. His hair was silver, but what caught me were his eyes. They were ageless, like deep pools of light blue filled with a love and depth that made me feel like I was in the Presence of Jesus, and I was overwhelmed by the sensation of purity and stature and greatness. He pulled out a crumpled brown paper bag from his pocket and slid an extremely worn, small leather bible from it. As he spoke his face lit up, radiating excitement, passion, humility, and love. Dima interpreted.

"I spent 14 years in a prison labor camp for preaching this book, and now here you are on Red Square and giving them away for free to all. See what God has done. I praise Him and I thank you."

I took his hand and held it and looked into his eyes. Actually, I couldn't stop looking into them. My eyes were welling up with tears. "No. Thank *you*, sir." I felt as if I had looked into absolute holiness and lived through it.

One afternoon we went out to a busy street corner and made two separate stacks of boxes. It was freezing outside. We had only one Dima that day, and he was a different one who was about 17 years old whom Rick had met. Rick and Gerry manned one station with Dima to translate, and I manned the other alone, with the Holy

Spirit. We began to draw passersby, and as I gave away a bible to one person, a crowd of 20 or 30 people encircled me. I looked the one person in the eyes and spoke to him, using a six-inch cardboard dove that balanced on the end of my fingertip to get his attention and use as an illustration. I had glued pennies under the outspread wings, which caused it to balance by the very tip of its beak on the tip of my outstretched finger. On its back and each wing were written the words "Salvation," "Jesus," and "Heaven," representing the seemingly impossible and invisible quality of Faith that causes those huge and eternal concepts to rest on my life, just like this bird with outstretched wings floated in perfect balance as it rested by its little beak upon my fingertip. As I spoke in English, I asked the man questions to see if he understood me, and he nodded and answered "Da," yes. Then I asked if he wanted to experience Heaven. "Da." I introduced him to Jesus, salvation, and heaven, steadily and lovingly looking him right in the eyes as I spoke. I continued this way with each person who would say yes to Jesus and receive Him, and then I would watch that person begin to glow as I gave him a bible; he would clutch it to his breast and I would pray for him, and then the next person would push into that spot as the first one moved back and drifted away down the street, smiling and glowing and embracing his bible. The crowd never diminished, and one by one a person would have an encounter with Jesus and then receive a bible as the others watched with rapt attention. Then as that one moved out of the circle, another would step forward, and others would be drawn to the outside of the crowd. I just kept looking into the eyes of the one, and a spark would ignite and that one would have an experience. The only words I could say in Russian were

Jesus, Bible, and Heaven, but the people absolutely got it and responded as if I were speaking to them in their own language. There was a strong sense of holiness and Presence and Heavenly encounter that thrilled me and kept me warm. When I ran out of bibles after three hours, the thick ice on the street had melted and we were standing in a puddle of ice water.

I could have gone on forever, I thought, but a woman interrupted us with a sense of urgency, and Rick and Gerry and Dima pulled me away and off to the hotel to get more supplies. We picked up some comic books in Russian we had brought that shared the gospel with pictures, and some stickers and balloons, and headed off after the woman on a quest I never fully understood until we got there. Something about children ....

It was dark and cold outside, and we followed her down streets and alleys for a while, and then she crawled through a gap in a high wrought-iron fence that sur-rounded a huge and impressive government-type building. It was all very strange and adventurous, and I hoped it wouldn't end in capture or death. It felt like I was in a spy movie. We followed the woman across the dark grounds and into the building through a back door, where the people inside seemed to know her. She took us up some stairs and down a hall, and there it was. She had brought us to a children's ward where the child victims of the Chernobyl nuclear disaster were kept. There were dormitories full of thin, white, bald-headed children. Leukemia victims. She stood in the middle of the room and smiled tenderly and motioned for us to proceed. *Wow. Oh, God, You do wondrous things.*

We looked around and started in on loving each

child. Dima was working triple time. We talked to them and hugged them and prayed with them for their healing and declared how much Jesus loved them. They received the picture books and stickers as if they were treasures, which caused their eyes to sparkle. We told them about Jesus, God's love, and Heaven. They all wanted to know Him. There were *rooms* full of these kids. I couldn't stop crying as I held each frail little body and kissed each hairless little white head. They began to smile and a light came into their pale, sunken faces.

"You're special. You're loved. You have value. God loves you so much He brought us all the way from America to tell you."

We were there for hours. I don't even know how we got home. I remember sitting in our parlor full of cartons of bibles and looking at Rick and Gerry, and we could hardly speak, except to express our gratitude for being permitted such an experience.

MOSCOW UNIVERSITY

Victor hated to be left out of our adventures and hoped we'd find places to go where we needed his cab. Moscow University, bastion of Communist thought, was one such place. It was surprising how many boxes Victor could fit into his car. Once while driving we were stopped by a policeman, and Victor enthralled him with tales of our adventures through words and drama, and then gave him a bible and blessed him. The cop walked away without giving us a ticket, opened the book, and began to read right there on the spot. I wish I knew what Victor had said to him.

We set up our boxes on the steps of a main building at the university and hailed each person who went in. There was a good response, and one professor gave his life and heart to Jesus right there in the open air. But it was freezing, and people were anxious to get indoors, so many hurried by. Thus we decided to set up inside the building.

There we found two grand staircases descending into either side of the foyer. Perfect. Rick set up on one and I on the other. As soon as the bell rang, we called out to the swarms of students: "Bibles, a gift, free of charge" in Russian. A crowd gathered around each of us. It was a major university, so there were some who spoke English. I met a wonderful atheist mathematician who gladly interpreted for me as I preached the good news of God's love from the steps in the main lobby of Moscow University. I knew it was the first time the gospel had been proclaimed in this center of atheism in at least 70 years. It was epochal. God showed up, people asked questions, and men and women encountered Jesus as we answered their questions and introduced them to a loving, personal God. Then the bell would ring, and many would run off to class, but some would stay. At the end of the next class there would be a whole new group.

The time between bells gave me a wonderful opportunity to deeply connect with my atheist math friend. I had read about a famous Russian mathematician named Ivan Panin, of whom he knew, and we discussed his work. Panin had written a numerological "bible code" sort of thing, and my friend was fascinated. We actually continued our friendship for several years and I sent him some literature. He was superb at gathering a crowd and introducing me. Then the preaching, teaching, and discussion would begin. It was there at Moscow University that I felt the pull to disciple Russia. Rick is an evangelist, to the core. But I am a teacher, father, discipler. I began to dream of setting up bible studies and gatherings for discussion and schools of the Holy Spirit. I felt as if I was living my destiny right there in the lobby, surrounded by curiosity and hunger and deep interest.

Then an extraordinary thing happened. We were out of bibles, but the discussions were still going on. I noticed a tall, pleasant-faced young man at the edge of the now rather large crowd, observing everything with interest. Then I clearly heard the Holy Spirit tell me to leave the group and go over and talk to that one man. He needed a bible. I struggled for an instant with the concept that it was better to focus my attention on the greater number, but I knew from experience that when God is moving on, the former things pass away and the anointing lifts. So I excused myself, and the students continued to discuss among themselves the things of God, piquing their own curiosities.

As I walked up to the young man and introduced myself, I asked if he would like a bible. His English was excellent and he was very interested, so I invited him to go out to the cab with me, where I had one bible in my backpack. He was extremely gracious and appreciative, delighted, in fact, and he began to tell me his story outside in the freezing cold, continuing as we moved back indoors.

His name, to my amusement, was Dima. His last name was Oryal, or something like that, which means "eagle." He had just been released from the Russian Navy and was on his way to greet his parents before beginning a job with the Merchant Marines on the Black Sea. As he passed through Moscow, he suddenly remembered a friend at the university and decided to stop for a visit. That's how he just happened to be in the lobby as we were sharing the Good News.

His grandmother had told him about God when he was little, and he had always felt His presence. But he described being in the Russian Navy as being like a tall, young sapling in the northern forest. All the pressures of the military and atheism were like heavy winter snow that weighed upon him and bent him over until he almost touched the ground. If he would bend and bend and not fight back, then he would not snap and leave his faith lying broken and crushed, buried under the full weight of the deep snow. He said my words were like a spring thaw; the sun had come out and now the snow was shaken off, and he was unbent and rising up, reaching into the sky again. He dramatized this by bending his arm down low and then springing it upright again. He told me many stories of his calling out to God to know Him from the deck of a huge ship; how he had felt that God was near but that he didn't really know Him and didn't know how to connect with Him. Dima felt there was some key he lacked to make that connection so the relationship could come alive and become more real. As we spoke and I introduced him to Jesus and the Holy Spirit, he felt himself coming alive inside. The very words seemed charged with life as they melted things inside him and stirred up old longings and breathed life into them. He had been searching for a real and relational God, and suddenly a new spiritual union was consummated. He felt as if he had discovered his life and his spirit had awakened from a long sleep. We talked at length, deeply attracted through love and admiration for each other, and exchanged addresses. He believed God had brought me all the way across the world just for him and this moment in time. I felt that if he were the only person I connected with in all of Russia, it would have been worth the whole trip.

SUPERNATURAL EVANGELISM

After the stadium rally of the summer, a number of churches had started up in the city. We connected with one and worked with it for the next three years. Our first experience there was on a Sunday morning in a theater auditorium where they were meeting. A visiting pastor from America was preaching, and I remember feeling embarrassed as I listened. He boasted about his huge building and large congregation in America. I sensed such a hunger in the assembly to hear of God's love and His goodness toward them. The preacher went on and on for maybe 45 minutes. When he finished, the local pastor stood up and spoke for five minutes about Jesus and asked anyone who would like to experience Him to come forward. The air was electric, and I caught my breath as a wind of the Spirit blew through the place. Suddenly the hair stood up on my arms and the back of my neck. A rush of about 400 people ran to the front of the auditorium, and the air became charged with the Presence of Jesus. I burst into tears and fell on my knees, having no control over my emotions. The pastor led them all in a prayer of repentance and surrender, and there was a kind of wailing noise mixed with sounds of great joy. Then the pastor asked all the ministry team and all the visiting pastors, including us, to come and make a kind of fire tunnel /

healing tunnel. Two lines of ministers faced each other and all who wanted healing walked through the tunnel as we laid our hands on them and declared God's goodness in a continuous flow of healing. It was profound, and one woman who was healed became a friend who later interpreted for us on other trips as well as having us in her home for a feast.

GREAT FAVOR

So many doors opened up for us supernaturally that we decided to rent an apartment in Moscow for a year (which became about three years). Rick would go as often and for as long as he could, and I would take teams from the church in Ridgway as often as I could. In 1992 we sent three or four teams, each staying a month. We continued to fill the apartment with bibles, at one point using the stacks of boxes for furniture. Rick told me once that in those years we all gave away 100,000 bibles! By 1993 we were moving away from Moscow, heading east toward the more provincial Russian city of Ivanovo, where there was a church plant; each time I returned there I got to teach in a new ministry training school started by the church in Ivanova to raise up Russian pastors. A whole chapter could be dedicated to those adventures.

We always took a lot of money with us for bibles and to give to Americans living there, as well as to rent vehicles for transportation, which increased to vans, and finally a Mercedes bus. We had to declare what we brought in, and I wanted to be completely truthful because the Favor of God was on us, and I didn't want to do anything to tarnish or compromise it or have to work from a place of deception. We would split up our cash, and on one trip, I personally was carrying $5,000 through customs and wrote it on the declaration. The queue was long, and cab drivers and con artists were all at the other end in a mob of people waiting to receive the passengers. The customs official was drunk, rude, and rather disheveled as he hollered at each one who approached him to stamp his visa. The man before me had declared several thousand dollars, and the official barked the amount at him so all could hear, and then said: "Show me." I watched as the man looked sheepishly around and then reached down into his sock and pulled the money out. All eyes were on him, and I prayed protection over him as he was released into the crowd. It was bizarre.

I was next. The drunken official looked at my declaration and said loudly: "Five thousand?" And when I nodded he repeated: "Show me." I'd been pondering what to do, but suddenly I straightened up and heard myself say in a commanding voice: "That's NOT appropriate!" He shook himself and looked blankly at me and then at my visa, stamped it, and motioned me on. The others on my team followed with no confrontation. I felt like the Holy Spirit had taken over, and when I told my Russian friends about it they were appalled. "That man could have had you arrested!" God is truly powerful.

Each time we arrived at the apartment we spent the first day talking to God, worshipping, asking God what we should be doing, and making our needs known. "We need a driver and a van, an interpreter, and we feel like we are supposed to connect with young people. We ask for those connections, Lord. Thank You, You are GOOD." Then we would praise Him and go out into the streets and on the metro (subway), and we would simply run into our Divine

117

contacts; but often they would find us! On one trip, on the first day, we met Denis, a young man who was apprenticing with the Russian Mafia, though we didn't know it at the time. It took us a little while, but we finally learned that that was how he was able to get us anything we asked for. First, he found a van to take the six of us around the city with boxes of bibles, but we soon outgrew it. Then we began to meet young people who wanted to help, and that's when we graduated to the Mercedes bus with a driver. I went with Denis to the vehicle compound to pick it up and was schooled in the fine art of Russian business. We went to five different offices, all on different floors of different buildings, each of which needed some money and a written request from me before they would stamp my pink sheet. Whenever I asked him about the logic or inefficiency of such a process, Denis would say with a wave of his hand: "This is Rosh-sha!" He interpreted for us many times during that trip and came to know the Good News of the Kingdom quite well, even asking me questions from time to time. He also had that uncanny access to whatever we needed. God was using even the Mafia for the benefit of His people!

The Russian teenagers who were attracted to us kept multiplying. A group of them hopped on the bus with us and told us they had made up some skits they wanted us to see. We barely knew them and were really flying by the seat of our pants ourselves, running into spontaneous opportunities every day, so we didn't pursue the issue.

Then one day Denis decided we ought to preach at his old elementary school. We loved the idea, but how could we make this happen? This was an era without cell phones, remember. Our bus driver took us to a large school where we piled out and entered the lobby. Denis went into the principal's office and later returned with her, a stern-looking woman in her late forties. When people speak passionately in Russian, it sounds as if they are arguing passionately. Hearing the principal and Denis yelling at each other gave us no encouragement. I thought that he had probably not been the model pupil during his school career and imagined we would be ushered out of the building promptly. To my surprise, the woman turned to us with a smile and said in English: "We shall cancel classes and have all of the students in the auditorium for an assembly, and then you may address them. Afterward you may address the teachers. Now, will you please join us for tea?" Having come from the American school system, we were overwhelmed by such a reception!

The six of us from America spontaneously dramatized several scriptures in a humorous and entertaining fashion, while Denis read them in Russian. Then the group of Russian teenagers who'd joined us on the bus asked if they could perform one of their skits. We barely knew them so I was a bit skeptical, but I sensed the Holy Spirit was leading so I agreed. They slipped into all-black clothes, pulled out a boom box, and rocked the house with a few choreographed pantomime numbers illustrating the power of sin and deliverance, all done with excellence. We were blown away, and the students loved it. We learned that Americans stand out in Russia more than we had realized – when those teenagers had seen that we were giving away bibles and sharing the Good News of the Kingdom all over the city, they must have learned from Denis our next place of outreach and simply shown up there, by metro or bus — eventually *on* our bus. They were part of the youth group of the church we had been connecting with. We counted ourselves blessed to have had them find us, and we would continue to work with them for the next year.

We shared the wonder of God's love with the school assembly, and all the students wanted to receive a bible and meet Jesus. Each of us went among them and prayed freely with them. It had been such a fantastic experience that we were asked by other teenagers to go to their schools, which began a tour of schools that would last for the next few weeks. But our conversations with the faculty were even more astounding. They openly confessed to not knowing anything about God, having been raised in an atheistic educational system. They were immensely interested in the bible and especially wanted to hear what we knew about the creation. Our discussions were wonderfully stimulating.

One day we decided to travel to the nearby smaller city of Podolsk, where Rick and I had had exceptional encounters at the open-air train station. Our team and the kids took the train, and Peter and I hired two cabs to carry us and the bibles; we raced over horrible, frozen, potholed roads at extreme speeds with drivers who smiled but knew no English. After several attempts at protesting the insane driving, I prayed loudly in tongues for the rest of the trip, looking at the driver wide-eyed and smiling as I prayed louder and louder. We beat the train to the station.

We set up our boxes of bibles on a large stage platform in the middle of an open square at the station. When the others arrived, we preached, put on dramas, and prayed for the sick. We'd attract a huge crowd and then pray with the press of people who wanted Jesus, bibles, and healing. We'd have a powerful time of connecting with as many individuals as we could before the train came, and then we'd start all over as the crowds would begin to arrive for the next train.

So many fascinating stories come to mind from those five years, but the overview is that we began to desire to get out of Moscow, which was rapidly becoming an international entryway into the country. Our desire was to work with the Russians in a smaller city, where we felt we could make a greater impact by working more in the Russian culture itself. A couple from our church, Peter and Anne, wanted to move there with their three children and work full time with a local church. We were working with the church in Moscow to set that up, but when we arrived that summer with a team of six adults and four children to help establish Peter and Anne, our plans dissolved and we suddenly had no open doors. We all sat in the Moscow apartment and prayed, worshipped, and asked God for a miracle. The phone rang. It was a man named Mark, who told us he was the pastor of one of the Dimas who had since moved to Ivanova, about six hours east of Moscow by overnight train, and that Dima was the main interpreter at the church there. Dima had somehow heard that we were back in Russia, and Mark was calling to invite us to join them in Ivanova. It was an instant answer to prayer!

Peter and Anne ended up living in Ivanova for nine years, had two more kids, and continued to work with that church. We returned with teams each year, and God continued to do outrageous things in the lives of people there. We held large outreaches in the main square, preached and taught in the church and ministry school, and worked with home groups and cell groups in the city.

HE IS JEALOUS FOR ME

Whenever I visited, I would run at full throttle for a month and I loved it. I particularly remember one summer night. It was about 11 p.m. and still twilight, and I'd been going since sunup. I had just finished leading a home group and was walking across the park toward the bus stop. I sensed the Presence and stopped. The Lord said to me: "Sit down on this bench." I did. I remember being excited, because that kind of direction from the Lord was usually what happened right before a divine appointment came along and a new relationship was birthed. *"Who is it, Lord?"* I looked at each person who walked through the park or who arrived at the bus stop. I enjoyed the cool of the night as I sat there, but no one stood out to me. Time passed and I talked to Him about it. Suddenly there was a stillness and a distinct sense that He was there, and He said: "It is I. I just want to sit with you alone for a while." I melted and was overtaken with wave after wave of Love and then overpowering Peace and then all-consuming Joy. It was wonderful. I spent the next few hours in the day-lit middle of the night with Him, the One who loves me.

VICTOR AND VICTOR

The long summer days in Ivonova brought folks of all ages outside in the evenings after supper. There is a park with an open square in the city, right by the river, where grandfathers told us they had gathered with their friends and families as young boys on summer nights, as their own grandfathers had, as far back as anyone could remember. We went there and met young people in their teens and twenties who were excited to practice their conversational English with Americans. Their teachers, on the other hand, later scolded them for the deterioration of their proper British English, and told them they were picking up bad habits. But we were delighted to find so many interpreters!

We'd learned many skits in Moscow from our teen-aged friends, and decided the square was the perfect place to try them out. I'd imagined gathering a small crowd in a corner of the plaza and drawing them in with our skits and then sharing a life-changing encounter with God with them and seeing where it would go from there. But one of our new Russian friends asked me, "Why don't you do it over there?" as she pointed to a huge wooden platform rising about five feet off the ground which commanded a spectacular view of the entire plaza. It was built out from the steps of a large government building which overlooked the park.

"What do they use that stage for?" I asked.

"Government officials give speeches and they have programs there on national holidays," was the reply. We ventured out onto it, stopping about a third of the way as it had a lot of give and sway to it. Although it was pretty rickety, we could see everyone in the square from the platform and decided to give it a try. We'd brought a boom box with cassette tapes that played the background music for our skits, and also had a microphone with a small portable amplifier. We donned our black pantomime costumes, turned on the amp, and cranked up the volume. One of our Russian friends announced that we were going to perform some dramas and invited everyone to enjoy them. A thousand heads turned toward the stage as we took our places and put on the music.

We performed my favorite skit, which illustrates how a searching young woman is being introduced into all kinds of life-controlling situations and then becoming ensnared and bound up in them, while being tormented and taunted by demonic beings. The prince of bondage and lies orchestrates the whole thing, until Jesus comes and offers deliverance. The dark forces kill Him, nailing Him to a cross, but He breaks the chains of Hell and Death and rises up to rescue the young woman. It was stirringly choreographed to the music and made a powerful impression. The youth pastor of the church we were working with then took the microphone and gave a moving message, telling how God's love reaches into our situations and circumstances to bring deliverance and rescue from all the things in our lives that control us. According to his estimation, about 400 people came forward wanting prayer for Jesus to come into their lives with hope and rescue. It was electrifying as we prayed in English with so many. Some of the youth translated, but there was too much activity for them to interpret every prayer and request; somehow God made up the difference.

In all of the excitement of the night I met many people, but two young men stood out to me. They introduced themselves to me when I had no interpreter, and though they spoke only Russian, their radiant, smiling faces beaming with joy spoke volumes as they told me their names were Victor and Victor. As I looked into their deep, bright eyes, I felt an immediate connection.

From that point on I ran into Victor and Victor almost every time I was out on the square. I began to realize that we were doing the same thing — we'd both be talking with small groups of people and end up bringing them into some kind of experience with God accompanied by joy, tears, prayer, and animated discussion followed by hugs and radiant faces. They were introducing people to Jesus! They didn't attend the same meetings we did, and I became very curious about them. I started running into one of them on buses, city streets, and in markets, but rarely did I have an interpreter with me when I'd see him. So we developed our own singular style of communication. I had a Russian-English dual-language version of the bible I always carried with me. I'd think of something I wanted to say to Victor and then look up a verse in English that I knew said something similar and show it to him on the opposite page in Russian. He would then respond. One time he was trying to let me know he had to leave, and he borrowed my bible and found the verse that said: "Then they all went to their own homes." I replied with: "Go and do likewise." We laughed and embraced as we split up.

The more I connected with Victor, the more I loved him and the more I wanted to know about him. I asked my friends to set up a dinner for us before I left Russia, and I purposed to have a translator there. Both Victors came to our apartment, and we shared a meal and I heard their story.

They had both grown up in Christian homes during the Communist regime and told me many stories about their life at that time. One of those stories especially impacted me. As a boy at an illegal house meeting, Victor remembered that one of the men spoke out a prophetic word in the middle of a time of worship — the Holy Spirit was telling them to turn off all the lights and lie quietly on the floor. Immediately they all obeyed. Soon several police cars drove up and stopped on the street. Officers surrounded the house and pounded many times on the door. From his place on the floor, Victor could hear the policemen talking outside among themselves as they cursed and declared that someone must have given them false information, that there was clearly no meeting in progress at this address. Finally they returned to their vehicles and drove off, as the believers quietly got up and peered outside and then proceeded to praise God with even greater fervor for this remarkable deliverance.

One of the Victors told of his experiences of harassment and abuse in the Russian Army, as he was tormented and ridiculed for his faith. But he also told of healing miracles he'd witnessed as he prayed for his tormenters and saw God heal them of various afflictions.

Finally I asked them how they had come to be here in Ivanova. They explained that after the Iron Curtain had fallen, both of them attended a newly established bible school in Lithuania. Upon graduation, they had prayed for God to show them where He would send them, as they felt they were to plant a new church somewhere in Russia. Victor received a dream in which he saw a city street so clearly that he remembered every detail of it, and he heard the word "east." So a group of young men started off on the train traveling east across Russia until they stopped in Ivanova, where he saw the exact main street he had seen in his dream. They disembarked and immediately began to pray in the city as they went about engaging in conversation with anyone they came upon. It turns out they had arrived at the same time we did, and that's how we met that night in the park as we shared the goodness of God and the Good News of His magnificent Kingdom, telling of it in two different languages, yet led by the same God into the same city. At that time Victor and Victor were holding their meetings in an apartment with a small group of Russians, but each time I returned from America I found that their church had grown; I even had the honor of being invited to preach in the rented building they had secured to house the increase of their fruitfulness.

All over Russia God raised up men and women with passion to spread the experience of His Kingdom throughout their land. I was privileged to be a tiny part of His work, as He drew many Americans to help equip the Russians to reintroduce their homeland to God's Love and His Truth and His Power. I could write an entire book dedicated to the exciting adventures I had over the period of those five years as I fell in love with the Russian people and watched what God did among them. *Do it again, Lord!*

Chapter Six

THE BREAD OF LIFE KITCHEN

THE RAINBOW GATHERING

The National Rainbow Gathering is an annual drawing together of 20,000 to 30,000 people from all over the U.S. and the world. They are people who come from many countercultures, including drug, punk, music and peace and love cultures, and from various backgrounds of holistic, Spiritualist and New Age perspectives. We camp for up to a month in a different national forest each year to celebrate life and freedom. The Rainbow Family of Living Light consists of all those who attend and all those who help to build a temporary "city" in the woods made up of many camps and villages. There is no limit to the creativity that is displayed and released there. It's a community that calls out *"Welcome home!"* to everyone, even the strays and rejected of society, and declares *"We love you!"* to everyone who arrives. The Rainbow Family actively pursues love, joy, peace, kindness, acceptance of diversity, family, community, spirituality, and freedom; they rejoice in the natural environment; they seek

129

healing for body and soul as well as truths and maybe even Truth; they embrace alternative cultures and lifestyles, creativity, expressions of beauty, mentoring in life skills, interchanging of ideas and wisdom, and everything that *"Eternity has placed in their hearts,"* as it says in Ecclesiastes. The Family has varying degrees of success at this, as we all do.

We have been a part of this gathering since 1992 as the Bread of Life Kitchen, because we value those same things and we see that everything being sought there is found in Jesus and the *now* experience of His Eternal Kingdom. We see that each person is highly prized, and *is,* in fact, the Treasure He is after.

BECOMING A KITCHEN IN COLORADO

By the early summer of 1992, I had been to Russia twice and sent two or three other teams over there. People in our little fellowship were growing in purpose and vision, and the church in Ridgway was becoming strong. One day I received a phone call from a woman in Paonia, a town about two hours to the north, where I had lived when I first came to Western Colorado. We knew a lot of people and had lots of old friends there. She told me that 20,000 hippies had descended on the Overland Reservoir, everyone in town was nervous, and the churches were freaked out. And then she asked me, "And what are *you* going to do about it?" Interesting question. I wasn't sure I was responsible.

"What am I going to do about it, Lord?" I asked. I wasn't ready for such a strategic response:

"Take seven of your people and go spy out the land."

Okay.

So eight of us got in a van and drove two and a half

hours north to the Overland Reservoir access road. There were plenty of vehicles parked everywhere as we approached the gathering. Pulling off the dirt road, we found an entire makeshift campground of uniquely converted school buses, vans, trucks, and older motor homes wedged haphazardly among the trees and bushes. The road was blocked to further traffic, so we left the van and hiked into the heart of the gathering, where we walked around the camps, met some sweet people, and had some great conversations. As we stood in a circle by the lake swatting mosquitoes, we prayed and asked the Lord what we should do, and He said: "I want you to come up and have Church Camp at the Rainbow Gathering this weekend." *Okay.*

We drove back to Ridgway and called on the church family to join us in a spontaneous all-church camp-out from Friday night through Sunday, and most everyone agreed. There were lots of families in our community with young kids, including our own. Because people had worked all day, we got up to the gathering around sunset on Friday evening, so we hiked in only a little way and decided to set up by the lake near the beginning of the trailhead, mostly in the dark and in the rain. We were a group who loved each other and loved to have fun, so we didn't let the circumstances rob our joy. Saturday we enlarged our camp, made corporate meals, and hiked around, getting into lots of conversations. Some of our people tried handing out tracts, but they were rejected for both content and substance, as no one at the gathering wanted to litter or carry around extra paper trash.

By Saturday night there were more of us, and we stretched several large tarps between the trees and made a campfire under them so about 60 people could stay warm and dry as the rain poured down for hours. That night we had a worship time with instruments and songs that lasted six hours, and a corporate experience of the love and Presence of God was manifest all around us. The singing continued in wave upon wave of worship and it seemed like it would never end. Finally, in the wee hours we quieted down a little as a holy awe seemed to overtake us and we felt the very nearness of God in our midst. We were still packed around the fire, with new people who had joined us to take shelter under the tarps. Then one brother quoted a scripture verse in the stillness. It was dark, with only the campfire's crackling flames in the center of a press of bundled-up campers. There was a pause, and then someone spoke out another verse, and then someone else another. We were listening, and then one by one we'd speak out whatever verse came to mind as the Spirit would prompt us. As we kept listening we heard a whole beautiful message being birthed and we were all the midwives. The Holy Spirit was weaving a breathtaking tapestry of God's love throughout the scriptures, and it was coming forth spontaneously from the mouths of many people. It was a sweet journey through the heart of God for His people and it was stirring us as we listened. Two young ladies by the fire began to weep, and someone ministered to them. God was doing something powerful, and we could only listen in awe. It was at this time that I heard the Lord commission us with the freedom to *BE* the Body of Christ at the Rainbow Gathering.

At around three in the morning we filtered off to our tents. And then the games began! Little did we know, we were camped right across the trail from A-camp. We didn't even know what that meant at the time. Alcohol is looked down upon inside the gathering by many because of the aggression and violence that often accompany its use and abuse. So our alcohol-drinking brothers and sisters are asked to make their camp on the outskirts of the gathering itself. And A-camp never sleeps. As we began to nod off, they proceeded to serenade us with foul, perverted, and blasphemous renditions of old church songs and hymns. One of our brothers had a vision of a huge demon rearing its ugly head in retaliation at so much heavenly grace pouring in to our camp. Their roaring went on until around dawn, when we all got a brief reprieve.

God tells us to bless and not curse. *How can we repay with a blessing, Lord?* We took over some fresh coffee and breakfast to those who hadn't passed out, and they were stunned. As we continued to bless them they responded well, and several times different ones among them would say, "If anyone gives you a hard time, just tell us; we'll take care of them." And I'm sure they would have. We made some friends that year who continued to visit our kitchen for years afterward.

That Sunday was clear and dry, and we shared food with many who were hiking in throughout the day. We stopped "trying to witness" and relaxed into *being* and found ourselves in great conversations, just loving people from all walks of life. By afternoon many of our folks had to return to Ridgway for work on Monday, but Linda felt strongly that we needed to stay and become a kitchen and feed people for the next two weeks. What does it take to be a kitchen? We'd come up for only a two-day camp-out and hadn't brought a lot of tools or supplies.

We found out we needed several things: we needed a

latrine dug a certain number of feet from the kitchen and from any water source. We also needed a compost pit and a grey-water pit outside the kitchen. And we needed a wash station for hands and one for dishes with three buckets in each: for soapy water, bleach water, and rinse water. Right then a tall hippie in overalls with a shovel over his shoulder came down the path and asked: "Are you a kitchen? Do you need a compost pit dug?" And he went to work. Then another barefoot young man stopped by and asked: "Are you a kitchen? Do you need some buckets?" And he gave us six five-gallon buckets. We didn't have much food, so a woman from Paonia brought us a big canner full of hot soup each evening for several days to get us started. And then the most extraordinary thing happened. Church people from five different counties began to show up with boxes of food, saying, "We heard we were supposed to bring food up to Chuck and Linda at the Rainbow Gathering." Every day bushels of produce and bread would appear, and we would make whatever showed up into meals. Each day it was like opening presents as we explored the new shipment. And the people kept showing up, both to help make the meals and to eat them. We were cooking in a couple of canners over an open firepit and on a two-burner, pump-up Coleman stove. Then someone gave us a heavy five-gallon cooking pot and we doubled our production. We ran out of fuel for the stove one morning, and by noon a couple from Cedaredge, about an hour away, came walking down the trail with two gallons of Coleman fuel, saying, "We were praying this morning and the Lord told us to take two gallons of fuel up to Chuck and Linda at the Rainbow Gathering." We were really glad the Lord knew where we were and what we needed, but were even more pleased that His people were listening and obedient. Everything we needed appeared daily: food, fuel, clean drinking water in five-gallon jugs, buckets, tools, toilet paper. Friends returned to help as they were able. And the beautiful people we had the privilege of feeding responded with lots of love and appreciation. We kept hearing: "We've been to the missions in the cities and they make us sit down and listen to the gospel and then they feed us. But you just love us and feed us. So tell us what you're into." "Yeah, who are you and what do you believe?" It was a huge wide-open door to introduce people to Jesus and tell them about the amazing Goodness of God! And we walked through it again and again.

I felt that the Lord had set us up, and He made it successful. We simply responded as He led us into His love encounter with the Rainbow Family of Living Light. We named ourselves the Bread of Life Kitchen and saw over and over the yearning in hearts to be loved, accepted, welcomed and affirmed, to belong and to contribute. Linda and I were the first Mama and Papa of the kitchen family, with Bruce and Nancy joining us that first year. Jody began to be pulled in a little more each year, and it took his wife Louise about six years to finally be totally drawn in, transformed, and immersed in the worship, and then she dove completely into the work with love. Rob and Barb showed up in Taos in 1995 and we fell in love with them. In Arizona in 1998 they too became fully part of the vision. After that we planned and prayed and traveled to the gatherings as family. We were all used to hard work, camping, building and inventing and creating, loving Jesus and people, and raising families. These four couples became the leadership and the heart of the kitchen

God began to give us favor at the gathering and among the larger Rainbow family. We spent years gaining credibility through our great food, excellence in our camp, loving service, and the Manifest Presence that made people feel safe and made the voices in their heads stop screaming. Unusual wonders and miracles began to happen, like food being multiplied regularly, water being supplied miraculously, mosquitoes and bugs disappearing, weather changing, and on and on. His Presence changed things as well as people; He began to draw many wonderful young people into our family year by year and He enlarged our hearts.

TRANSFORMATIONS IN WYOMING

Every Rainbow Gathering is unique and affords at least a hundred stories. It would take a whole book to tell all that God has done at the Bread of Life since 1992. As well as miracles, there are themes, lessons, breakthroughs, graduations, and seasons. And then, all the stories are about *people*. There are several from the Wyoming gathering in 1994 that stand out in my memory.

We had set up our kitchen in an upper meadow that year, apart from the main meadow and off the trail, and it was rural and quiet. People knew we were a Christian camp, and in those first years that was often tested. Nudity is common at the gatherings, and we had decided that we were not there to judge anyone and definitely not to argue. In fact *"No Arguing in the Kitchen"* was our first and, for a long time, only rule. One day I was serving an afternoon meal from behind the counter. By this time we had graduated to 20-gallon pots and propane stoves, and we'd built a strong lodge-pole framework in the trees to support our tarp roof. It was a beautiful Robinson Crusoe-style fort in the woods. A woman came across the meadow toward the kitchen with her bowl in hand for a meal, and she was wearing nothing above the waist. She was basically flaunting herself as she walked up to the counter, waiting to see what kind of rise she could get out of the Christians. I smiled and welcomed her as I looked right into her eyes with the love of Jesus. The eye is the lamp of the soul, and I looked into hers with love and compassion. I served her some food and spoke to her with warmth and respect. She began to ask me questions, and as we conversed I asked her how she was doing. She was emotionally hurting, and I introduced her to Linda, who has the most tender heart for the hurting. They talked for probably an hour, and Linda hugged her before she left. Later in the day the woman returned with her tent and backpack, asking if she could camp with us. She was fully dressed, though her lack of clothing had never been mentioned. We've gotten to know her and seen her at many gatherings since.

She helped out at the medical tent, which at the gathering is called CALM, an acronym for Center for Alternative Living Medicine. One night a freaked-out young man was taken into their tent. He had been dosed unknowingly with an hallucinogen and had suddenly begun to experience it while he was in the woods as night fell. He thought he was going crazy, and his screams drew some people to him who helped take him to CALM. Our newly dressed friend happened in just then and said: "Take him to Bread of Life. They'll know what to do for him." So they did.

We were in the kitchen, sitting around the campfire,

when an entourage of night travelers burst in with an extremely shaken, paranoid young man. We sat him in a chair in front of the fire and gave him some tea. He was wild-eyed and dodging firebolts, periodically jerking around and trying to describe what was happening, but it was changing too fast for him to keep up with, so he sounded incoherent. We gathered around and laid hands on him and began to pray. Peace began to invade his drama, and within 15 minutes he was in his right mind and thanking us for saving his life. A psychedelic trip normally lasts about six hours. It was definitely miraculous. We introduced him to Jesus, and he stayed in our camp for days. It turned out his name was Free. Jesus gave him new meaning for that name.

BUMMING A CIGARETTE

We met Zach in Wyoming. He came into our camp with his guitar on his back and sat down and played hymns and gospel numbers. He knew a lot of Christian songs, yet he wasn't a believer. We didn't have regular musicians in the early days, so we welcomed his playing. He was helpful, too, and was especially willing to assist me in the many projects I had going. We dug a latrine together in some hard soil, and he never complained or wanted to quit. I liked him and had some good times with him, but whenever I started to talk about Jesus or asked Zach about his relationship with God he would clam up and sometimes even walk away. Apart from that, he usually stayed close by me.

When we left the gathering we gave a number of folks a ride south, and Zach was one of them. We stopped just before sunset at a Pizza Hut and treated all our guests to supper, the first one in two weeks that we hadn't cooked ourselves. Just that made it immensely enjoyable. As I left the joking and the laughter around the table to step outside and make some adjustments in the camper, I noticed Zach and Linda talking out by my truck and I walked over.

"That was a great meal. I was just telling Linda how much I'd like a cigarette to top it off," he told me.

As he was speaking I noticed a cook come out the back door of the restaurant, and he had a pack of cigarettes rolled up in the right sleeve of his white T-shirt.

"Hey, he's got some cigarettes. Why don't you go bum one?" I said, a little excited at the impeccable timing. Zach looked down and shook his head.

"Why don't *you* go bum him a cigarette?" The Holy Spirit asked me. Interesting question.

I knew Christians in Colorado who would vehemently assert that it was the devil speaking, but I knew the voice of my God, and He was always up to something good. Sure, I can do that. So I walked over to the cook, who was dumping trash into the dumpster, and asked him if I could bum a cigarette. He gladly pulled out the pack. And right then a young hippie couple ran up and asked him if they could also have cigarettes. The gentleman was generous, and even lit theirs. *"Please don't ask me to light it, Lord."* I silently prayed. And He didn't.

As I walked back to Zach and Linda, I noticed he was upset and speaking to her. She put her arm around him and loved him.

"Here's your cigarette," I said cheerily but cluelessly. "Hey, what's up?" He was crying. And then Zach's story poured out.

He used to go to a church and had really loved it. He got involved, and that's where he'd learned all of those songs. But things went sour and there was some abuse and hypocrisy and a whole lot of hurt, and Zach walked away. Like many others, he thought the Rainbow Gathering was the last place in the world where he would have to run into Christians. But when we showed up he watched us and got involved, and he got close to see if we were real. He didn't want to talk about it; he wanted to see it lived out.

"I was just telling your wife that when you went over to bum a cigarette for me I couldn't believe it. You, a *pastor*. I just broke down. It caught me off guard. I feel like you think I'm more important than appearances. Like maybe I can believe that God loves me, and that you can love and accept me." Huge walls seemed to come crashing down just then, and Zach surrendered his pain. It was triumphant. We all cried. And I thought: *"God, I never, ever would have thought of that. That You would use a cigarette! You're amazing. You love relentlessly and You are unoffendable. I want to be like You."*

ALL-NIGHT DRUMS IN OUR KITCHEN

We heard about a regional gathering in late September of that year in the Four Corners area of Colorado, only a few hours from where we lived. Regional gatherings are much smaller than nationals, with less than 1,000 people, and much more intimate. Fall Equinox in the Rocky Mountains can be pretty cold, so we went well prepared. We took some new folks with us who had never been to a gathering, and they were not from a hippie background. We're all mountain folks and very experienced at camping, so our scene was kind of like a glorified hunting camp. The nights were cold and we had lots of food and hot tea and coffee; we were pretty popular. But when the rains came and we had the largest dry space at the gathering, we were overwhelmed — even overtaken and overrun.

It was dark and we were trying to serve dinner, but every square foot in the kitchen and around the campfire was taken up by bodies. And as the rain continued, wet campers continued to stream in and squeeze into the warm space. Kerosene lanterns were burning and the fire popped and crackled, we passed out hot stew, and the crossfire of conversations swirled around us in an ever-increasing din. Laughter and joy, noise, food, and smoke. And then the drums started. Every third hippie at a gathering has a djembe, or hand drum, and there were almost a hundred hippies under the tarps. The first to be served supper were finished, and the drum skins were warming toward the fire. And then the beat began.

One of the things we've learned to do that keeps the atmosphere in our camp positive is to control the music. We try to have someone playing throughout the day, with whole groups jamming on drums, guitars, flutes, and whatever else we have available during our busiest times and corporate gatherings, bringing worship before God and filling the camp with His praises. Back at the Four Corners we didn't have a single musician, and our small team was completely outnumbered. Drumming at night — *all night* — is what people *do* at gatherings, and they were starting to do it in our kitchen. Now, some large drum circles are known to be trance inspired, and crowds of people dance naked around a huge bonfire all night, fueled by drugs and adrenaline and whatever spirits they are open to. But this was *our* space.

The steam coming from wet clothes was mixing with the smoke in the camp. And then a couple of women sitting cross-legged by the rocks in front of the fire started to pull off their wet outer layers. And then their shirts. Their bare skin shone in the glow of the flames as they moved their arms in the air, dancing from the waist up to the beat of the drums. Topless. Our new folks were freaked out and they kept coming to me and asking what we should do about it. Can't we stop it? I talked to the Lord and He told me just to love and serve. So I told the team that since they weren't comfortable with what was happening, I'd like them to just pray and intercede. If they didn't feel they could stay, they were free to go to their tents and pray there. They were still going to hear everything that happened — you can't get out of earshot of a drum circle at a Rainbow Gathering! Especially when it's in your camp.

Only Bruce and I remained in the kitchen. We were definitely outnumbered. I told him our commission was only to love and serve and he agreed. But after midnight we put away the coffee and started serving Sleepy Time Tea. The drums had quieted a bit, and there was more conversation around the fire. The crowd had thinned out and I think the rain had even stopped. They started telling stories. They were all religious or anti-religious stories, and there were a few there with the intent to draw us into arguments. They mocked and blasphemed, made fun of

Christian practices, and glorified occult experiences. Bruce and I had to bite our tongues, and a few times we had to extricate ourselves as we slid into some wide-open arguments. But I clearly heard the Lord tell me not to say a word each time I asked, and I'd find myself looking at Bruce and quietly shaking my head when I'd hear us getting sucked into a debate. This went on for hours, and there was a certain tension in the air.

At three in the morning that extraordinary feeling began to creep in, where quiet stillness starts to displace a long celebration, and people who've been involved, extroverted, and interactive for a long time begin to slow down and isolate into introverted silence. You could hear the crackling of the fire. It became peaceful. All eyes were watching the flames moving among the glowing coals, and occasionally a burned-out log would collapse into the firepit, sending a burst of sparks upward. In this quiet pre-dawn space, a young woman spoke up:

"I think we need to apologize to you guys. We've been in your camp, eating your food and drinking your tea and staying warm around your fire. It's like your home, your living room. And yet we've been making fun of what you're all about. It's not right. We've been disrespectful of you and your beliefs, yet you just keep serving us and showing us love. Where are you at? What *are* you all about?" You could hear the proverbial pin drop.

And then I heard Him whisper in my heart: "Now. Tell her." Every face turned toward me and everyone was completely attentive. I felt the Spirit well up inside me as I spoke:

"I've done some pretty rotten things in my life, and I

143

deserve to be judged for them. I deserve judgment. But what we believe is that Jesus came and took all of the judgment I deserve onto His own body when He died on the cross, so I'm free from judgment. And I'm free to be loved. He was innocent and He took my guilt and now I'm free. But I also believe that I can take all of the judgment I think you deserve and place that on the body of Jesus on the cross and let Him die with that. Then *you're* free from judgment. Then I don't have to judge you and I'm free to love you. You're free to be loved."

There was a murmuring around the campfire of "Ho" being repeated from a dozen or so mouths. It's hippie for "Amen." And then her story came out. She'd grown up in a Christian home, but it was very legalistic. When she got older she rebelled and rejected the lifeless religion and the harsh taskmaster god. But there was one problem. She'd fallen in love with Jesus as a little girl and loved the connection she'd had with Him in prayer and in the bible. Since she couldn't comprehend how that loving Jesus could be a part of the harsh, judgmental, performance religion she was fleeing, it left a place of unreconciled confusion in her heart. She'd just stuffed all that confusion deep inside. But *Jesus* wouldn't stuff. She ran into the love and acceptance she found in the Rainbow Family, and found it to be much more real than the verbal attempts at love that she'd received from people in her old church whose unloving attitudes had contradicted their words. Where was Jesus in all of this? She didn't know.

"For the first time I feel Hope. I see that you guys can live in this world and in the Rainbow, and you are living the love and you have Jesus. I don't have to give Him up. You've given me Hope, and I'm so grateful," and she began to quietly weep. There was a holy hush, punctuated with a few softly spoken "Ho"s.

But it was soon broken by the cynical rebuttal of a Navajo man. "I can't believe you guys! You can snowball them with your Jesus and your God, but your God and your people came and wiped out my people and you destroyed everything we value in the name of your God. I believe in White Buffalo Woman. She's the one who will come back and set things right on the earth. You can have your lies and your hypocrisy. You killed my people for your God, and I won't believe in that kind of God."

Silence.

"You're right," I said. "My people destroyed your people and that is wrong. My white ancestors and my Christian ancestors lied to, stole from, and cheated your people. They raped your women and killed men, women, and children, justifying it with lies. They worked to wipe out your entire culture. Those are gross sins and deserve judgment. And I confess them to you as sin and ask, even beg your forgiveness for every wrong my people perpetrated against your people. I am so sorry; please forgive me for the sins of my people against you." And I knelt before him weeping.

He began to shake and weep. "No one has ever said that to me before." We looked into each other's eyes and embraced. You could hear the "Ho"s punctuate the silence all around the tent. It was powerful. *You set this up, God. Thank You.*

It was approaching dawn and we all stood up and hugged and said goodnight as we headed out of the kitchen in different directions, as friends now. We'd been through something holy together and it had left its mark. Bruce and I debriefed for a while at my camp before I lay down to worship my glorious Living God, as I overflowed with love and gratitude, awe and adoration before I slipped into a sweet, short sleep.

Later in the morning the Navajo man came around. The Native Americans I have known have been a particularly stoic group — loyal and perceptive, but not showing emotion at all. He came by me and greeted me, but didn't speak much. What he did, though, was stand right beside me for most of the day. There was an honor in it that I felt very strongly, and it went way beyond words. It felt like friendship extended and embraced, like covenant and commitment, like "Whatever happens, I've got your back. Nobody messes with you." It felt good. Like generations of dams had burst and the river was flowing again. *Thank You, Jesus.*

And this gathering brought a breakthrough for us into the hearts of some of the long-time Rainbow family members, the influencers. There was a new credibility gained and a new level of favor and respect. I was talking to one elder and our conversation was about discrimination and acceptance. I told him: "The Rainbow family accepts everyone without judgment, except for born-again Christians." He didn't even use his trump card, that it's the born-agains who judge everyone. He just said: "You're right, and that's not okay." And then he asked my forgiveness. We were building bridges.

GUTTER PUNKS

The Oregon gathering in 1997 was in a tight, hilly

place and extremely crowded. We got there a little late and had a hard time finding a good spot for our camp. After walking for miles over the site, I'd seen only one spot I'd felt drawn to, but it was taken. The younger members of our Bread of Life family often joke about how we as elders use the Holy Spirit to sniff out the perfect spot, and they are partly right. We were almost ready to settle for a location that wasn't perfect, when I asked if we could stop and pray one more time and then go back to the spot I'd liked at the top of the hill. We paused and prayed, and when we climbed the hill we saw that someone had packed up all their tents and moved them elsewhere. Why, they'd just been saving the spot for us! It was a great gathering.

Some of our closest neighbors were a group of gutter punks. They were very young and wore all black, punctuated with silver spikes and studs; and they were especially dirty and had spiked hair, some of it multi-colored, and lots of piercings. Several of them had arrived before us and had made a very creative and organic tree-bark, cave-like shelter at the edge of our camp. We pretty much took over the hill, but we served great food, so as their friends filtered in and their camp grew, it was convenient to have a good kitchen next door. Plus, we dug the latrine.

Every morning as Jody and I served breakfast, we noticed these kids wouldn't look at us or respond. So we devised a plan. When they stuck out their bowls for food, we'd wait. They'd wait. And when nothing plopped into the bowl, they'd look up. Bam! That's when we'd hit 'em with the full-on love, smile, eyeballs looking straight into eyeballs, I see you and am gonna love you and you can

147

have as much food as you want, but first, I'm gonna ask your name. "What's your name?" When they told us we'd work at remembering it. And we'd give them an extra big helping.

The next time they came around, we called them by name with love and affirmation and told them how glad we were to see them. We just drenched them with love. They were quite used to rejecting and being rejected, and I'm sure the being rejected had come first and started the whole cycle. But if they were to reject first, it wouldn't hurt as much. We simply refused to receive their rejection. I know we were a little obnoxious to them at first, but the coldness really began to melt away and they started *responding* to being greeted and welcomed back with joy, to being told someone was glad to see them again, glad they came over for a meal. Someone thought they were special and beautiful and talented. It was really fun, and they started calling us by name, and then even greeted us first. They were looking us in the eyes! I loved it.

Jody was working with a couple of them, and I had a few of my own. But my real interest was in Devon. He had *Leader* written all over him, and the others treated him as such, though he couldn't have been more than 20 years old. We started having conversations that were quite stimulating, and one night I sat down on the ground beside him and we ate supper and talked. He stayed until well into the night, which honored me as it meant he was missing some of the outrageous nightlife at the gathering, one of the main attractions for many of the young people. But he wanted to talk and I was glad to listen. I was functioning on an immense overflow of the Love of God that wouldn't quit. It just poured out of me and into him.

After a while he asked me some questions, and I shared my story and some of my encounters with Jesus with him. Before he got up to go I gave him a pocket-sized Gideon New Testament with Psalms and Proverbs. He was interested in it.

But it blew my mind when he returned in two days and told me, "I read that book you gave me."

"The whole thing?"

"Yeah. There was a part I really liked. It says: 'He who walks with wise men will be wise, but a companion of fools will be destroyed.' I've always dreamed of being a wise man, but I see I'm hanging out with fools and acting like one." We talked for hours and I told him he could meet Jesus, that He is the source of all wisdom. He was truly interested; he'd never heard any of this before. He wanted to process it and come to grips with true wisdom. I looked at him with such joy, and with the Father's pride in the son's wholehearted quest after wisdom and truth. His whole countenance changed, and he left the gathering with a new hope. I committed him into the hands of Jesus and I've thought about him many times, but he's one of the people I haven't seen again. Yet....

AUTHORITY OVER FLIES
AND MOSQUITOES

Even the thought of a gathering on the Northern Peninsula of Michigan had us picturing swarms of mosquitoes and stocking up on bug dope. We were right. The site was by a beautiful river, great for swimming on the hot, humid days, but there was no good drinking water and the flies were atrocious. And it rained for days and the mud became slippery clay. We slid-hiked in and found that all the main kitchens were camping across the river where they had also established the main meadow. When we crossed the river on a makeshift bridge, I became strangely nauseated although I'd been fine earlier. As we searched the woods we found all the good sites had been taken, and we saw nothing that looked like it would work. When we went back across the river, the nausea immediately left, and I had the clear feeling we were not supposed to camp on the other side. So we spread out through the woods looking for the perfect spot. After about an hour, several of us converged in a beautiful meadow surrounded by trees, a short walk from the main trail. There was a cluster of tall pines in the middle of the meadow that were the exact distance apart to hang the ridgepole for our kitchen-roof tarps. In all ways it was perfect, except that it was so far from the heart of the gathering we wondered if anyone would come to our camp, which was important, as we had a lot of food and had placed an order in town for more produce. So we prayed several times and each time the amazing Peace came over us. I was sure God was telling us to camp there, even if it made no sense. So we hauled our equipment in.

Setting up camp is a three-day process of packing in many dozens of gurney loads of supplies each day, cutting dead timber for ridgepoles and posts, and building the fort. I love that part. But it's so much work and time that we have to commit fully to doing it, and we kept having these nagging doubts. Peace came with prayer; doubts came when we thought about it. Let's see ... the good news is that God isn't a God of doubt. So we put doubt aside and plowed ahead.

But then there were the flies. And the mosquitoes. There were times when we would stand still, or when we were perched in a tree tying off a ridge pole and couldn't move, and we'd look and see swarms of flies covering our skin. I have a photo of Tobias so covered it looks like he's wearing a suit of flies. It was gross. Finally we'd had enough. We got together and took authority over the flies and mosquitoes in Jesus' name. And they left. Completely. That was it. People would come into our camp and ask where the flies were. Rumors spread throughout the gathering, and people would stop me when I was out on a supply run and say: "I heard you prayed and all the flies left your camp. Just like Moses." Right. Actually Moses called them in, but then they left when he prayed and God withdrew the plague. Anyway, ours were gone.

But the strangest thing happened next. The Forest Service came in and evicted the entire gathering from the other side of the river. All the kitchens had to break down and move to our side. It had something to do with its being an archeological site. The result was that we were at the center of the entire gathering, settled into the best meadow on-site. All we had done was to obey God and He had set us up. Proverbs 3:5 became freshly alive and real to us:

"Trust in the Lord with all your heart,
and lean not on your own understanding;
in all your ways acknowledge Him,
and He shall direct your paths."

151

WATER FROM HEAVEN

Water was the next problem. The river was so full of sediment that its water plugged every filter in minutes. Many of us searched for water sources and devised filtering contraptions, but nothing was successful. The entire gathering required water from town. Vehicles were set up for water runs, and fortunately the town, curiously named Watersmeet, was not far away. The grocer's brother owned a car wash with unlimited water from a prolific well, and he offered the water for free to the Rainbow family. He'd moved from Southern California to the Northern Peninsula and wondered where he'd ever find any excitement. And behold, it came to him. He was thrilled and spent much time at the gathering with his new friends. The grocer made extra income by ordering food for the gathering at cost plus ten percent. We ordered all our produce for the Bread of Life from him, and he gave us some great deals. Our water use as a kitchen was so high that we had to make a trip to town every morning just to keep up, so Jody and I alternated driving his old red Suburban packed with five-gallon jugs inside and on the roof rack. Because it was a water-run vehicle, and because we were camped near CALM and had four-wheel drive so that it could also be used as a Medivac vehicle, we were able to drive into the gathering, past all the checkpoints, and right within yards of our camp. This really helped with hauling the full jugs of water into the kitchen by hand each day, as it was only a short trip from our new parking spot. Jody actually got to drive out a heart-attack patient and I took a woman in labor up to Bus Village. She almost delivered in the Suburban; she had a healthy baby girl only five minutes after we brought her up the hill and helped her into a converted school bus belonging to her friends who'd fixed it up into a sweet home.

As the crowds increased during the last week leading up to the Fourth of July, our water use increased, as did the people walking on the trails and roads, so we'd leave very early in the morning to avoid foot traffic. One night we simply ran out of water, which shut us down from cooking, washing, and drinking coffee, tea, or water. Plus it affected the morning start-up for the whole kitchen, which would have to wait until we returned from the water run at around 10:00 a.m. So we prayed. We weren't really praying about the weather at all, and we definitely weren't hoping for rain, as the roads had just started to dry out, but we asked God to fill our water containers — all together as a group in agreement.

It's remarkable how fast the weather can change. Suddenly there was wind and huge dark clouds appeared, and then came thunder and rain. Like that. We raced around the camp collecting all our five-gallon buckets and 20-gallon cooking pots and placed them everywhere the water was pouring off the tarps that stretched over our roof. And they filled fast. We had to stay on top of switching them so they didn't overflow. And when we had filled every container we could find, the rain stopped. It was exceptional.

The five-gallon water jugs, all 30 of them, were sitting empty outside the kitchen with their lids screwed on, waiting to be picked up for the morning supply run. We couldn't catch rainwater in them because of their narrow spouts, so we ignored them. Water was being heated in the big pots for washing and boiled for drinking. We were back in business. But when Jody got up first thing the next morning to carry the jugs to the Suburban, he found that all the jugs with their lids screwed on were full of water! No one had filled them with rainwater and no one had gone to town. God had filled them, and it was fresh, clean drinking water! We were amazed.

As we marveled and praised the Lord, a guy stormed into our camp in a rather angry mood and shouted at me: "Quit messing with the weather!"

"Hey, I didn't ask for rain. I just asked the Lord to fill our containers with water. You'll have to talk to Him about it. Oh, and did you hear? He even filled all our jugs that we left outside with their lids on!"

"You guys are nuts," he said as he walked off. Yeah, a little bit, I guess.

FOOD-LINE HEALING

I love serving food to people. Especially at the gathering where everyone is hungry. Walking everywhere and living outside in the mountains are sure ways to build up an appetite. Plus, people take psychedelics and stay up all night and forget to eat, and by the time they make it to a kitchen that's serving a meal, they are ravenous. Most people aren't even picky at that point, but we strive to make outrageous meals that will blow their minds and set their taste buds dancing. And we have a protocol for serving — you've got to be filled up with God's Love and overflowing until you can't stop smiling, then you look into their eyes as you serve them a bowl of elk-steak fajitas, or grilled salmon in a pasta salad, or sweet-and-sour duck on brown rice, or homemade falafel, or fresh fruit salad, or fresh vegetables in tabouli, and then you speak a blessing over them and hand them a gift from the heart of God and the heart of the kitchen. It's not just a good meal, it's an *impartation* of love and nourishment. It's great fun. And people are so grateful, there's always plenty of affirmation and appreciation coming back to you.

Jody and I love to serve, and sometimes we mix it with prophecies. When we see people who are sick or hurting, we'll stop to pray over them for healing. One morning a young man was in the food line coughing and looking really ill. When he got up to the counter and asked if he could have some breakfast, Jody said: "No." And when the guy looked up at Jody with a puzzled expression, he added, "Not until you let us pray for you." So he said, "Okay." We prayed, and then he walked off into the woods with his bowl filled. It's happened thousands of times. But I remembered him.

Later that summer a friend of ours from Denver called with an inspiring story. Her daughter had been at a large outdoor meeting in a downtown Denver park and had heard a young man up on the stage share a story of God's love. He said he had been at the Rainbow Gathering and he was really sick. The doctors had spoken a sentence of death over him for an incurable disease, and he'd gone to the gathering for one final blowout party. He went to the Bread of Life Kitchen for breakfast and two guys prayed over him before they filled his bowl, and he walked off into the woods and God healed him right on the spot, and he gave his heart to Jesus right there on the trail. We were so excited just to hear about it. Thousands of phenomenal things happen every day, but we don't always get to hear the end of the story. It was superb to have some feedback and it encouraged us immensely.

God's always working, and sometimes we get to be a part of it; I love hearing about the good fruit that comes after we have prayed. It's so encouraging. *Thank You, Father*.

DRUM-CIRCLE DELIVERANCE

There's a lot of spiritual energy at a Rainbow Gathering, to say the least. And there are a lot of spirits there, as there are everywhere. Not all are holy or good. At late-night drum circles you can encounter all kinds of spirits, depending on where the inspiration is flowing from and where the energy is going. We all make choices every day for Life or Death. I've been at some outstanding drum circles that are celebrations of life and joy, and at some that are celebrations of sensuality and lower carnal desires, and also at some that are just really dark. I want to share two stories that illustrate some of what is happening in the invisible realm.

A friend of ours was at an all-night drum circle and she didn't know Jesus at all. Suddenly He appeared to her in a vision, and as a result she surrendered her whole life to Him. She's been walking with Him ever since.

One young man was drumming in a large drum circle around a huge bonfire as he had many times. It was late at night and things were getting pretty intense and trance-like. He looked up and began to see demons around the firepit. As the drumming increased in intensity, he became more and more terrified. Finally he fled the circle and started running down the trail through the woods in the dark of night. As he passed other camps on the trail, he saw frightening creatures and heard shrieking noises. At the entrance to some of the camps the creatures screamed at him and tried to draw him into those camps, and he ran faster. As dawn approached, he finally heard what sounded like birds singing beautiful harmonies in the night. He stopped and was drawn toward the singing; as he approached the camp he felt safe, and a blanket of peace filled the air. People were playing softly on guitars and worshipping God, and they welcomed him in. Through the experience he came to know God's love for himself. He had entered the Bread of Life Kitchen.

PURE LOVE

Evenings at the Bread of Life are impressive. There's usually an outstanding meal that draws hundreds, served with love by beautiful people; there are lanterns lit and glowing in the twilight, musicians jamming, campfires starting up, kids running and playing, and all our dinner guests sitting in clusters on the ground, on logs and stumps, some in camp chairs, and many gathered around the fires. We used to have one campfire under the kitchen roof, but we outgrew that and have had many other configurations of three or four fires, or a long semi-circular pit, all with the purpose of gathering more people around the fire's warmth on chilly mountain nights. As everyone bundles up against the cool night air, the after-dinner hour usually progresses into a time of worship as more musicians gather, folks snuggle in around the flames, and people release their love songs to the One who loved us first. It's a beautiful, free, and holy time. It can be a meditative time filled with deep wonder, or burst into spontaneous explosions of joy, or anything in between.

One night as I was standing outside the kitchen leaning on one of the supporting poles, a man sidled over.

We were enjoying the overflow of the music and singing and the general atmosphere of family and love. A conversation started up and he said to me:

"I see things. I see auras and spiritual energy."

"That's cool," I replied.

"No, really. I can see the colors of energy. I see what's happening here right now."

"I understand."

He continued, "This is *pure love!*"

"I know!"

"No, you don't understand. I can *see* the energy, and it's pure love. You rarely see it as pure as this, like I'm seeing it right now."

"I understand. It's good isn't it?"

"I don't think you get the importance of this. The light — it's pure. It's emanating off all of these people and this whole tent. It's *pure love*."

"I know. I love it. And it's happening because it's Jesus. We're worshipping Jesus and He's here in the midst of us. *He is Pure Love*." He looked at me with skepticism mixed with curiosity and shook his head from side to side. I smiled hugely and looked back at the radiance in the worship tent. He hung around in the background for a while that night.

Sometime the next day he came back to talk. He helped me work on a water-filtering device, which leaked horribly under pressure so that it regularly drenched us, spraying our T-shirts and shorts, and leaving streaks of wet dirt down our bare legs and feet. As we shared the soaking, laughs, and ideas about water purification, he began to open up. He told me he "saw things," things in the unseen realm, and sometimes he saw things that were going to happen and then they did. He'd have dreams, and then they would unfold in life around him. He asked what I thought of that, as a Christian. I spoke to him about the spiritual realm and about spiritual gifts God gives us, even when we don't know Him or understand their purpose. They are like jewels planted in our path, and when we respond with curiosity we follow their trail and find that they lead us to the treasure chest. In that chest are limitless treasures that reflect the King; they are the treasures of His Kingdom. And though they are a delight to explore and play with, the true goal of the whole adventure is that we meet the King and learn from Him. We sat on overturned five-gallon buckets behind the kitchen at the edge of a grassy meadow and talked for over an hour about the spiritual world and how it works. He was open and humble and very interested, and my goal was not so much to instruct or correct him as to encourage him that God had given him gifts and that he was being led into an encounter with the Giver. We were talking freely and looking into each other's eyes with joy and excitement as we realized new dimensions of God's love.

Suddenly I saw a shadow pass across his face and his whole expression changed. He began to spout some religious rhetoric that didn't come from his heart, and I watched the metamorphosis with wonder. As he was speaking, my attention was drawn to a huge bumblebee riding the summer air as it hovered around him. Then it shot up the leg of his baggy shorts as he sat on the bucket. I grimaced as he jumped up clutching his crotch and let out a horrendous shout of pain. Still shouting and grabbing his crotch, he did a kind of cross between a hobble and a gallop out into the meadow, swearing and shaking his head. And then he turned around and did the agony gallop back toward me.

"I believe in signs," he croaked. "Everything we were saying before was the truth. The last part that I said was bullsh__!" And he galloped away. I fell backwards off my bucket and lay in the grass laughing for 20 minutes!

Chapter Seven

MULTIPLICATION OF FOOD

ELK-STEAK FAJITAS FOR 400 ~ AGAIN

I can't remember when it started, the first time we saw the miraculous multiplication of food. It seemed so natural, like it was the most obvious occurrence one might expect at suppertime at the Bread of Life Kitchen. I do remember holding a bowl of some gourmet fare as I walked out along the line of over a hundred people queued up for the evening meal.

"Preview of coming attractions," I declared as I sampled a bite while I showed off the chefs' creation and let folks sniff its aroma.

"Loaves and fishes, loaves and fishes," prayed a happy camper as he raised his eyebrows and smiled at the banquet in my bowl. "Amen!" responded a dozen others.

And then it started happening. We'd look at the

161

length of the line of hungry people, then look into the 20-gallon pots, and all the kitchen help would agree in prayer: "LORD, MULTIPLY IT!" It happened at gathering after gathering. And though we always prayed for it, we grew to expect it. And though it always occurred as we had expected, we always had to deal with the marvel of it each time we'd prepare all the food that we could until it filled a pot. We'd watch hungry campers stream in for hours filling our lines as we'd serve a seemingly limitless amount of food from a limited-sized pot. I just never lost the wonder of it. I can vividly remember one occasion.

We had some visitors from Colorado who had never been to a Rainbow Gathering. They attended a church that was loving and outreach-oriented but didn't see much of the supernatural works of God or the supernatural gifts of His Spirit. They were curious, though, as they had heard stories about the Bread of Life for years. One of the men helped me for hours as we prepared the elk steak and stir-fried it with onions, peppers, and spices in a rich marinade we'd concocted. We talked and bonded in the bustling kitchen as the drums and band played outside and people who had heard the rumors of "elk-steak fajitas at the Bread of Life" continued to fill the meadow around our kitchen. The music played, people danced, children ran in and out, and the fires were lit as the feast came to the climax of its presentation. We prepared two pots, one with the elk steak and one with sautéed portabella mushrooms for the vegetarians. The dinner guests queued up as the counters were spread with bowls of grated cheese, salsa, and sour cream, and the grills began to turn out hot tortillas. As the festivities continued we all prayed our happy mantra over the pots: "LORD, MULTIPLY IT!" Then we called all the kitchen crew and the musicians and all our guests into a moment of silent expectation, soon broken as one of us shouted out a prayer of thanks to the One who gives us every good thing. And the crowd roared, "AMEN!"

I was serving the elk that night and I told my friend from Colorado who had helped me cook that he should take a burrito now behind the counter, as the line looked to be about a quarter-mile long. He is a gentleman and he refused, declaring that he couldn't eat knowing that it was impossible to feed so many with the limited amount we had made.

"No, I promise you, this happens every time. Everyone will be fed. He always multiplies it; no one goes without." He didn't believe me. Unfortunately I don't think he ate at all that night, and it was delicious.

I remember that one night so well because I was serving the elk and Jody was serving the mushrooms and we both had the same experience. As the line continued to increase, the food continued to decrease, until we could feel the scraping of the stainless-steel spoon on the bottom of the 20-gallon pot. I looked in, and it was *low*. My immediate thought was that I should lessen the portions to make it last longer, as I peered down the line of guests and its end was nowhere in sight, disappearing into the woods. But something rose up in my spirit that said: "NO. My God is a God of *Abundance!*" And I laughed as I heaped out generous helpings onto each tortilla, scraping the bottom with every flourish. Interestingly and without communicating, Jody and I both decided to partially cover our pots with their lids and not look inside as we scooped out the delicious contents, so we would not think in terms of the limited quantity of the food inside, but only of the

163

abundance of our Father. The food held out for hours until everyone was fed, and some even came around for seconds. That's how amazing our God is!

MULTIPLICATION OF MONEY

It was a hot and muggy drive across the midwest to the Northern Peninsula of Michigan in our old Suburban in the summer of 2002. The air conditioner was shot, it was the end of June, and all the windows were wide open as we rolled down the highway. Linda, who loves to swelter, was lying across the back seat sweating in the airless heat, while the rest of us practically hung out of the four front windows. There were four vehicles in our caravan: a couple of passenger cars and the two Suburbans which pulled trailers filled with our kitchen gear, food, and supplies. Our Suburban had a CD player, but we could barely hear it with the roar of the highway.

I was driving and I remember realizing that we still needed $1,000 to meet all of our needs. I handed the young man who was riding shotgun an envelope filled with hundred-dollar bills.

"Would you count these and see how many we have?"

He pulled them out and counted. "Eight."

"No, we need ten. Try it again."

Again he counted: "Eight."

"No, we've got to have ten." Four times he counted, slowly, licking his fingers and pulling the bills apart, one by one, and he came up with eight each time. "One more time..." And on the fifth count there were ten! How does He do that?

ABUNDANCE ALWAYS

There are countless ways the Lord has provided for us, but it's always with benevolent extravagance and supreme bounty. Whether it's water, food, wild game (elk, salmon, venison, wild boar) or money, it always comes when we need it. For quite a few years we received a lot of support from a few churches and individuals. But it seemed that as soon as we began to depend on them, God would change everything. When we were on the road to the New Mexico gathering in 2009, we had only received half of our usual budget; this was the first time that had ever happened. So we decided either God was up to something new or we wouldn't need as many supplies that year, for whatever reason.

We'd ordered our bulk grain and supplies from a food co-op and had them packed in the trailers with our equipment. The caravan took off from Ridgway heading south, planning to stop at Sam's Club in Farmington, New Mexico, for all of our produce before continuing into the mountains to the gathering site. You've never really traveled until you've been on a Bread of Life supply stop at Sam's, or a fix-the-trailer-lights adventure in a Wal-Mart parking lot at ten p.m. Our caravan from Farmington to the Rainbow Gathering consisted of eleven vehicles and three trailers! I've forgotten how many people that included.

Sam's Club is a massive discount warehouse of bulk equipment and food that has huge flat-bed rolling pallets you can fill up with about $1,000 worth of groceries each. Linda's a great planner and shopper, and she kept a team of about eight people loading four of those carts with supplies while I took care of gassing up vehicles and some other business. When I went back into the store they were all in line at the register. I knew I had $2,200 in my pocket and that it was the last of our money. As I looked at the four mountains of groceries, I began to feel my heart race and had a little trouble breathing. Two of them went through the register, a monumental feat in itself, with the scanning, counting, boxing, and reloading. And then *bing!* The register rang up $1,800. Two full carts remained. Do we abandon them and split? Scan until we reach $400 and leave the rest of the pallets for them to restock? Somehow we decided to run both carts through the register and see what happened. I'm often the Man of Faith of the hour, but I didn't feel it at all in that moment. I was sweating and squirming. One of the gallon cans of sauce tomatoes from one of our many cases had a dent and rust on it, so I decided to run it back to the shelf for a replacement. I needed some space.

"God, I know You are a God of abundance and here I am thinking only in lack. That's wrong and I know it. Forgive me. I'm going to declare it right now in the face of all circumstances: You are the God of Abundance! In You there is No Lack!" Peace swept into my soul with a rush of fresh wind and I began to laugh as I felt complete confidence take over my emotions. I returned to the register with my can of sauce tomatoes.

The final cart was running through and the team was beautiful to watch and fabulously efficient by this time, loading, re-stacking, packing, and balancing. They all stood at attention and smiled at the finished job. The cash register rang it all up and the final sum appeared: another

166

$1,800! I paused and mentally counted the $400 in my pocket. Just then my cell phone rang.

I answered to hear the voice of my friend, another Chuck, who had driven from Pagosa Springs to meet us here in the Sam's Club parking lot to join us for the final leg of the trip. He'd brought a team from his church as well as some folks from the International House of Prayer in Kansas City who would be part of the Bread of Life crew this year.

"Hello, Chuck! We just arrived. We're outside in the parking lot and we see all your rigs. Oh, and by the way, I've brought $1,400 in cash to add to the budget. Would you like me to bring it in now or just give it to you when you come out?"

"Wow. Right NOW at check-out stand 12 would be super great, Chuck. Hey, I'm really glad you made it." *God, You're amazing!*

People kept showing up in our camp with more money over the next few weeks, which enabled us to make several more supply runs into town, as well as pay for the gas to return home. But God did two more miracles on that first night.

The first one involved the trailer lights. It really wouldn't be a normal trip for us if we didn't have problems with them on the road. We tried to get them working in Farmington, but with no success. It was getting late so we decided to take off in the hopes of making it to the Forest Service road and being off the highway before dark. It didn't happen that way. But what did happen was that I received a call on the cell phone shortly after dark from the car behind me that my lights were now working.

Would I like to test the turn signals? They functioned perfectly and we had no more trouble with them!

The second miracle involved the logistics of finding a place off the narrow dirt roads of the national forest at midnight large enough to accommodate eleven vehicles and three trailers, where about 40 of us could camp for the night. We never want to arrive, as we once did, at the craziness of the "Welcome Home" site at a gathering in the middle of the night. On the trip out of Farmington, Bruce was driving the lead Suburban, which was pulling a trailer, and I was riding shotgun. We really hadn't thought much beforehand about how impossible it would be to find a suitable site, but as I peered into the darkness of the deep black forest beside us looking for an intersecting road, a turnout, or a wide space in the road, we began to discuss it. We'd seen nothing. Jody and a few others called to ask if we could stop to camp. *Okay, Lord. We need a REALLY BIG space where we can all pull off the road safely and camp.*

"Wait, Bruce, stop here! I think I see something. Let me get out and check it out." I hopped out with my headlamp on and scouted the terrain. The other vehicles each came to a stop behind us, a long line of headlights extending back into the night. Some of the folks got out to look around. And what we saw was *the* most perfect place imaginable! A wide drive turned off the road to the right and descended a small incline, opening into an enormous circular meadow surrounded by a log-rail fence. The place was so huge that all of our fleet could pull off the road and circle up, leaving room to turn around and easily get out in the morning. On the other side of the fence was a grassy meadow with a lovely babbling stream running through it.

There was plenty of room for us to spread out large tarps on the ground, and everyone could sleep outside who wanted to. When we turned off the headlights, we were thrilled by the breathtaking display of stars; the whole Milky Way lit the sky above us and the thin high-altitude air and absence of any other lights allowed us to see about ten billion stars. At least!

We awoke after daylight and fired up a stove for coffee, and we all took our time getting up. Around nine a.m. we had our first morning meeting of the gathering, and many of us really met one another for the first time, heard each other's hearts, and shared our dreams and passions. We pulled out a guitar and drum and worshipped together as a team and asked God for vision for the adventure ahead. Family bonding had begun.

As we were worshipping, a couple of Forest Service cars pulled up, and a few of us went over to do diplomatic business with the officers. Another good reason we wanted to be off the road in the morning is that the law enforcement officers can often be very picky; at some gatherings they have given numerous tickets to the Rainbow people. The vehicles that arrive at gatherings are often not completely legal, and every seat belt, turn signal, license plate, etc. becomes an opportunity for a citation at least, and a vehicle search at worst — people don't usually leave their drugs at home when they go to a gathering.

We were excited to find out that our camping spot was entirely legal, *and free!* We honored the officers and made friends with them, and they supplied us with a map of the whole area and showed us how the gathering was laid out and where to go, which was extremely helpful. Our God looks out for us!

169

MORNING MEETINGS

When we first started the Bread of Life Kitchen, and for probably six years afterward, we had around ten people on our team and were constantly running at full throttle, never having time to all sit down and talk, love, process, and focus. The late-night crew heading for their sleeping bags might meet the breakfast crew at dawn at the changing of the guard, and then not see one another again until noon. But around 1998 that began to change, when people we had fallen in love with at previous gatherings began to show up again wanting to participate. The four core couples were established by this time, and we found that the hungry people we were introducing to Jesus each year were hungry for love and family as well. Plus we began to attract a large group of young people who wanted more out of life than they were experiencing: more love, more intimacy and honesty, more spiritual reality, more daily adventures, more of the Life of Christ manifesting in supernatural experiences, more joy, and more encounters with a living "church without walls" that was ever-present around and within us. That's when we started having morning meetings. Our team grew from ten to 150 over the next ten years.

The morning meeting is a curious, organic phenomenon. The early-breakfast team goes to work at six or seven a.m. By ten o'clock the 20-gallon pot of oatmeal may be finished, in which case a second breakfast is underway: pancakes. At around ten we'll blow the shofar, which is a ram's-horn trumpet from Israel, or the conch shell, which blasts at a much lower pitch. This is to gather the tribe for the meeting, but especially to wake up the late-nighters still in their tents. The gathering of the clans takes a little while. First the musicians start in with hand drums, guitars, flutes, a harp, banjo, voices, and whatever else is available. Singers and dancers join in, and the still-sleepy take a seat in the circle with coffee cups in hand. The music jam might be a rousing boogie of exuberant praise, or a more meditative expression of heartfelt thanksgiving and worship. Every day is different.

But the main purpose of the meeting is *connection* — to connect with God and each other. It's a time to hear what happened the day before and what's happening in our lives. It's a time when people stopping in for breakfast or cruising by the camp can be drawn into the family. It's a time for loving each other. It's a time when we focus on what we're doing as we're doing life together. And for the leaders it's a time to guide, teach, and coach the family through the drama of the events of the day and of life. To the church, it sometimes looks like a front-lines, hands-on training school. And sometimes holy chaos. We've seen physical healings, demonic manifestations complete with deliverance, and supernatural encounters with Jesus that caused people to surrender their lives to Him. We've had baptisms, weddings, and intercessions. There have been times of teaching with role-playing and questions and answers, times of weeping, and times of rejoicing. There have even been times of great Holy Spirit exuberance that erupt in outlandish displays of joy and surrender — those are the times when the ground may be littered with bodies rolling in laughter or simply "blissed out" and soaking in the beautiful Presence and Glory of a Living God who touches our spirits, souls, and bodies in powerful personal ways, refreshing us, renewing us, and often healing us inside and out.

One morning in California in 2004, 75 people had joined our morning circle. When the Holy Spirit began to move among us in a way that stirred our hearts intensely, some demons became stirred up as well and left three men yelling out strange things, croaking, and writhing on the ground. Two of our crew started to yell back at the first demon, commanding it to come out. The noise had begun to attract inappropriate attention, so my goal was to get our guys to quiet down and start dealing with the *person* rather than the demon. It soon seemed that they were able to handle it, and they walked the man away from our group and dealt with him more privately and with tender love. I moved to the next guy. He was now lying pretty still and some folks were praying over him, so I figured we could more fully deal with him later. I went toward the third fellow, who was lying on his back on the ground, snarling. Young men were commanding the demon to come out of him in a rather authoritative and composed manner, so I decided to watch and see how they did. As persistent as they were, there seemed to be no progress, only a continued inhuman writhing from the man on the ground, punctuated with a few strange verbal snarls. I looked and saw a vision of a snake. This young man was not a Christian and I knew he was exploring shamanism. He had come to our "Divine Guidance and Dream Interpretation" arbor by the side of the main trail the day before. There he'd received some "words of knowledge, words of wisdom, and prophecies" (as described in First Corinthians chapters 12 through 14 in the bible) that had really spoken to him, and he was now more curiously hanging around our camp and liking the strong sense of spiritual community he felt there. I looked into his face and asked him to open his eyes and look at me. When he did I locked into his gaze, and when his eyes would start to roll back into his head I would call him back. I looked into his soul with the love of the Father and I got him to stay with me with only a few interruptions.

"I'm seeing a snake. Do you know what that means?" I asked him.

He seemed pretty surprised but curious as he nodded his head in affirmation. I looked up at the crowd that had gathered around us and spoke to him: "I'd like to take two other guys and go over into the woods with you and talk about it if you think you'd like that." He agreed.

As we sat in the shade of the aspen trees, he felt relaxed and opened up. He told me that only a short time before he had gone through a shamanistic ritual and had asked a snake spirit to come into him and be his spirit guide.

"Would you like to renounce that and break the agreement you made with that spirit and be set free from it?" He didn't know how that could happen as he thought it was a rather permanent commitment, but he said he would like to. I told him about Jesus, and about how He came to break every curse and set us free from every binding stronghold that the demonic realm may place us in. "Jesus has come with a power and authority and Kingdom that supersedes all other realms and governments, and His power to set one free is greater than any oath or incantation, or the rule of any dark force." He was interested.

I let him know that Jesus had come to restore to him the authority over his own being to choose whom he wanted to obey. He could no longer be held prisoner to any spirit or captive to any lies. We began to ask the Holy Spirit to show him some lies he was believing so that he could choose to accept or reject them of his own free will. As he saw and rejected these lies, we asked him to tell us what the truth was. He saw it all pretty clearly, even the admonishment that he must fill the space that he had given to the snake spirit with the Spirit of God so that no other spirit could move into the vacuum. He'd had a major breakthrough. A few days later we baptized him with a dozen others in our morning meeting.

We also baptized the young man I'd left lying on the ground, as we were able to take him through a similar deliverance. The baptism was unique in several ways. There was no river or swimming hole at this gathering, so we made a rather coffin-like bathtub of logs and tarps to immerse the folks in. In his letter to the Romans in the bible, Paul describes baptism as entering into the death and burial of Jesus, as we receive what He did for us in a dramatic, prophetic encounter, going down under the waters of death and rising up into newness of life. We also asked each person to choose a spiritual mother and father from our camp to do the baptizing. Many of these young people have had very negative experiences with family and parents, and we wanted to show them the love and affirmation of true parents as we invited them into a new, very extended family. Each mother and father spoke a blessing over the "new creation" before they dunked him or her. We honored the fairer sex by baptizing them first, as we didn't change the water — a precious commodity — and everyone had been camping in their clothes for about two weeks. The water did get a little dark, but everyone was too elated to notice.

The same young man who was delivered from the snake spirit grew in his relationship with Jesus; he returned to the gathering the next year and fell in love with one of our spiritual daughters. Another year later I married them at the Rainbow Gathering in a full-on festival wedding celebration in a meadow near our camp, complete with a chuppah — the beautiful cloth for the bridal canopy spontaneously supplied by some Israeli friends from Jerusalem Camp — bagpipes, drums, dancers, and all their friends and family. The bride even arrived in the meadow on our gurney, famous throughout the gathering for hauling food and supplies in and out over the rough trails. It has a single motorcycle wheel in the center and front and back handles for the operators. In this situation it was covered in white cloths and the bride sat on top dressed in a beautiful gown, while two brothers pushed it across the meadow to the waiting crowd of rejoicers. In one year I officiated and attended nine weddings of our spiritual children. Now they're having babies.

FOURTH OF JULY, RAINBOW STYLE

The Fourth of July is considered by the Rainbow family as the high holy day, the culmination of a full week of partying, *and* the only day when there is *QUIET* from dawn until noon. That alone makes it one of my favorites. For the first time in weeks you can awaken at first light and discover that the all-night thundering of several hundred distant drums ceased sometime in the wee hours. Suddenly there are no drums at all, not the distant drone, nor the close-up beating out of rhythms in the next camp. And there's no talking, shouting, screaming, hollering, banging on pots and pans. You can actually hear the birds singing! It's so still when you wake up that it seems you can even hear the forest growing.

Thousands gather in the main meadow on that morning to silently meditate and pray for peace in the world. I love to go there and quietly intercede for the multitudes that flow in slowly and steadily from all the camps throughout the morning, like streams filling a huge meadow until the dam breaks and it overflows back out into all the world. I'll sit against a rock at the edge of the meadow, soaking in the Presence of God and wallowing in His Love. When the Spirit prompts, I begin to silently and respectfully walk among the worshippers, praying for them to receive revelations of Truth and have encounters with God, to discover His purposes for them and to fulfill their destinies. I weave through the crowd, moving toward the center of the meadow where the "peace pole" stands. It's eight or ten feet tall and decorated with flowers and icons, especially with Native American, Buddhist, and Hindu items but with many diverse and unusual things as well, and an occasional picture of Jesus or a Celtic cross. This peace pole is the focal point of the meadow and of the inflowing multitudes who are spread over an area of several acres.

I feel my commission is to bring the Presence of God on-site, first by *being* an open Heaven myself. With the Spirit of the Living God inside me, I can expand that portal of life within and around me to encompass a much greater area. The bible tells me there is a *River of Living Water that flows from deep within me* in the gospel of John, chapter seven. So I draw on it, play with it, and watch the wondrous things God does as I walk among the silently meditating ones. I can *feel* the meadow changing! My goal is to fill it with Heaven and an outpouring of love that is greater than what is already there.

I was deeply involved in this at one gathering when I felt the Holy Spirit lead me to move in ever-smaller spirals into the middle of the meadow, right into the center where the peace pole stood. I arrived at one spot and was directed by the Spirit to sit down. There I continued to release light and love and hope and quietly declare His goodness. Suddenly my eyes were opened to see what was happening in the invisible and heavenly realms. I saw that there were a lot of different spirits being drawn to the assembly. And I saw a young couple walk into the center by the pole with their naive hearts wide open, their arms outstretched, ready to receive any spirit that might be available to them, thinking that *"it's all good."* I saw a huge dark form moving through the air toward them and its shape began to morph so that its forward part became similar to a funnel-like tornado that aimed itself like a spear tip right at the heart of the young woman. *"Oh no, you don't. Not on my watch!"* And I raised my arm and a sword shot out with laser-like intensity, blocking its advance. I prayed and Heaven opened up and an angelic host flew down, creating a barrier between the dark forces and the people worshipping around the peace pole. Then I invited revelations of Truth and of Jesus to come to those people, bringing hope and promise, thrilling them with visions of their purpose and destiny. There was a battle raging in the heavenlies, and many times I lifted a Sword and Shield in the Spirit to block a demonic being from entering the unsuspecting ones, and in its place I invited the Holy Spirit to fill them with the Knowledge of the True and Living God. The intense warfare lasted about

177

three hours. It was extremely exhilarating, exciting, and constantly challenging. There was a great angelic host around, and I saw things I'd never seen before. And I was the one who *wasn't* tripping on psychedelics!

At midday the greatly enlarged assembly that radiated out from the peace pole like a mandala of living souls spread out to form a gigantic circle of thousands of diverse people who held hands in unity, completely encircling the main meadow. Some years the number is so great that they become a chain of tiny shapes on the crests of the surrounding hills, an encircling army silhouetted against the blue sky. In Montana in 2000 I stood in the center and heard the Lord say, "Look up," and as I did so I saw such an encircling army, and then He said, "These are My end-time warriors." In Michigan in 2002 I heard Him say that He was displacing unrighteous authority and replacing it with righteous authority. He loves these people and has such plans for them.

When the circle was complete, someone began the "Om" and it was picked up and then it swelled, then rose and fell in waves of corporate humming. This continued as a carnival procession of costumed revelers made its way from Kiddie Village, across the main meadow, and into the heart of the gathering where the peace pole stood. Most of the children at the gathering were in the parade, many with their parents. There was a celebration of the future generations, and as they came into the meadow the Om crescendoed into an explosion of noise and cheers, and the games began. Watermelons were carried in by hundreds of porters, and food was distributed throughout the throng. As the day heated up clothes were removed, people tripped on various psychedelics, and the culminating party of the entire gathering was underway. Drums were brought out and dancing and celebration continued until dawn.

At the ʻUtah Gathering in 2003, a large group of believing Christians in the main meadow interceded throughout the quiet time. When the carnival exploded the silence and the drums erupted around the peace pole, we were all together in the center and one of our sisters began to chant, "Nothing but the blood of Jesus!" as hundreds pressed in to the center and took up the chant, and the drums beat to the rhythm of the song. It was an outstanding prophetic moment, though I'm sure many did not consciously understand what they were doing.

On those Fourth of July days when I've engaged in such intense warfare, I generally leave when the party begins. I'll grab a slice of watermelon and retreat from the revelry back to the relative peace and quiet of our camp. That day in California I returned to the Bread of Life and knew that I was emotionally drained. I ran into Brad, Aaron, and Jody, three of the papas of the camp, and as I hugged them I realized that I had two options for refreshing and renewal after the rather draining battle I'd fought. I could go to my tent and take a nap. Or I could get drunk in the Holy Spirit with these brothers. Instantly I chose the latter, and we collapsed into a pile of bodies in the dirt, rolling and laughing until we couldn't get up. I heard a voice from the kitchen shout out: "Why are the elders sitting in the gate?" And then he answered himself: "Because they can't get up!" And the camp erupted in rounds of laughter.

Being in such an undignified state feels great, but I don't always want it to occur in so public a place. An afternoon meal had just begun to be served and hundreds were arriving to partake of it. It was well beyond our ability to control our raucous and drunken behavior by this time, and I barely noticed the reactions. Religious spirits got their hackles up, timid souls who didn't understand such antics were either curious or offended, or both. Some folks laughed and rejoiced, and the freedom-loving rowdy Rainbows loved it, later commenting on our ability to be free and happy without the slightest tinge of stuffiness. But from my place on the ground with twigs and leaves stuck to my clothes and hair, and dirt everywhere, I have sometimes had momentary flashes of desire to be somewhere hidden, tucked away in the woods where I'm happily not a spectacle. It passes quickly, and I never remember it the next time when the explosion of Heavenly laughing ecstasy hits. As the apostle Paul said in Second Corinthians 5:13:

If we are out of our mind, it is for the sake of God;
if we are in our right mind it is for you.

or in "The Message":

If it seems that we are crazy, it is to bring glory to God.
And if we are in our right minds, it is for your benefit.

I love reveling in the Father's delight in me as I frolic with the Holy Spirit and look more deeply into the glory of Jesus, intoxicated with His love, as it takes my attention off myself. Paul says again in First Corinthians 4:9:

... for we have been made a spectacle to the world, both
to angels and to men. We are fools for Christ's sake ...

I can pull off a degree of appropriate composure and

180

decorum when needed — I think. But people ask, "What is the fruit of such shenanigans?" Initially, it's that I really like them, and I feel the Father's pleasure in me. That's advantageous in itself. But I also had an experience in Wyoming in 2008 that gave me fresh insight. Jody and I were "drunk in the Holy Spirit" in front of the kitchen, once again, right before dinner. There was a pastor there who had come to the gathering in 2006 in Colorado and been part of our kitchen for the first time. He had since suffered a nervous breakdown and had been in deep depression for such a long time that he had to give up the pastorate of his church. He came for a variety of reasons to the gathering in Wyoming, but one of them was that it is a place of spiritual energy and the Bread of Life Kitchen a place of great safety, power, and healing. Jody and I were "out of our minds" for God, or completely "toasted" when we saw him in his fragile state and without reservation assaulted him with our love and joy, tackling and embracing him enthusiastically. As we laughed over him something broke. The oppression lifted and didn't return. He was changed; he was in his right mind. It was wonderful.

RAISED FROM THE DEAD IN WYOMING

It was a Fourth of July in Wyoming in 2008 when I was again walking and praying, releasing and interceding in the main meadow. I made a wide circle around the area and moved silently through the crowd, feeling the Father's love and the Presence of the Holy Spirit as I worked my way slowly toward the center of the crowd. Near the peace pole I felt the Holy Spirit prompt me to sit down, and as I began to respond I felt as if He said, "No, about a foot back." I moved back and sat down on a broad clump of grass and began to glory in God's Presence, worshipping Him and experiencing a Heaven that was wide open. Glory and Majesty, Grace and Goodness, Joy and Life streamed from the heavenly realms into the meadow, and I felt waves of rapture wash over me. In the midst of my reverie I sensed a commotion beside me, and I opened my eyes and turned my head. A man was lying there with several others leaning over him, one searching for a pulse while others tried to shake him and another performed CPR, but with no results. They were pretty frantic, and I sensed it was a drug overdose, but I was amazed at how everyone maintained respect for the silence! They worked to revive him for quite a while, but they finally climbed off him, looking badly shaken.

I was full of the Spirit, fully loaded, and I saw his foot lying motionless and cold right beside me. I reached over and held it and spoke "Life," and Life just poured right out of me and filled him, and he breathed and then sat up! The men jumped back from him, and he shook his head and looked around. I looked back into the Lord and asked, *"WHAT was THAT about?"* He answered and said, "I'm calling these people who are dead into LIFE." I was soon caught up in the Spirit, and though I had intended to talk with the man, when I was able to look around again he had gotten up and walked off through the crowd. I ended up worshipping some more. This was the third time I'd prayed for someone who was dead and they'd come back to Life.

MAIN MEADOW HEALING REVIVAL

Often we hold our corporate worship time in the

main meadow on the third of July. We prepare food for the main circle and a team of us takes it down on our gurney about an hour before sunset. This in itself is a major event.

First, the kitchen crew spends hours creating an exotic tabouli — a colorful and bountiful array of fresh vegetables diced and stirred into a bed of bulgur and then mixed with a dressing of lemon juice, olive oil, and large handfuls of herbs and spices. Live, fresh vegetables are a delight at a gathering, where rice and beans are often standard fare. Our tabouli is placed into two 20-gallon pots with lids and then bungeed to the four-handled, single-wheel gurney for the long ride down the trail to the main meadow. Next, the musicians, revelers, porters, and servers gather for the procession, with guitars, hand drums, voices, and long-handled serving spoons all becoming the joyous musical clamor of a celebration in motion. Two strong men become the gurney drivers, with the man in the rear controlling the hand brakes on the downhill stretches. It's a rollicking, joyous parade along the busy trail filled with foot travelers as we play, sing, laugh, and connect with the hordes of diners heading to Main Circle for the evening feast.

We burst out of the woods into Main Meadow to the sound of the conch shell being blown, calling in the thousands of people who arrive from all directions, their bowls, spoons, and cups in hand, gathering for the evening meal. The kitchen crews arrive with huge amounts of prepared food in a wide variety of containers — old ice-chests, 5-gallon buckets, metal cooking pots, and 50-pound brown paper flour sacks that contain thousands of warm bread rolls from Lovin Ovens, freshly baked in their many unique ovens built from 50-gallon drums encased in rocks and mud and heated with wood-burning fires. The servers with their food gather in the center of the huge circle around the peace pole, where we line up for washing as a woman trickles bleach-water from a gallon jug over our hands.

The thousands of diners are ushered into two gigantic concentric circles surrounding the area where the servers are waiting. The pair of concentric circles face each other, about four feet apart, to allow the servers to pass between them with carts, wagons, or on foot to scoop out food into the bowls and plates on both sides. Bringing your own bowl and utensils is *a must*. Experiencing the dynamics of this enormous nightly feast is *a joy*! Toward the Fourth of July when the crowds quadruple, we sometimes have several pairs of concentric circles rippling out from the center to contain the larger numbers.

We eat family-style. Once the food servers are ready and the people are all seated, a conch shell is blown for attention and the town criers shout out their announcements as they move around and holler into the crowd. These announcements contain various health, safety, and event issues important to the gathering as a whole. Someone is selected to offer a prayer of thanks or a moment of silent blessing or an Om, and the entire assembly is called into a single focus for a moment in time. This occurs with varying degrees of success, as there is always peripheral noise, but I'm often amazed at the focal energy that is generated at this time. Twice I've had the honor of giving the corporate thanks at Main Circle, and both times I was rocked by the vastness of the open Heaven that was manifested over this huge assembly.

Serving is a great joy. The dinner orchestrator will send the kitchen teams to different points around the circle to start the process. Two strong young men will carry one of our pots by its handles as they move in a clockwise direction between the seated rows. A server will go before and one behind, scooping the contents into bowls and plates on the right and left as the musicians and singers go fore and aft. We connect with the people with love, complimenting, making eye contact, joking, and laughing as we make our way around the circles. It's loads of fun, and many of our folks love to be part of the serving team.

In New Mexico in 2009, we finished serving and began to gather on the outskirts of the dissolving dinner circles as the sun was just beginning to set and small clusters of people moved about the meadow. We put on some warmer layers against the cool mountain night and pulled out instruments, as musicians from the other Christian camps joined us to form a circle of about 50 people, praising God as the sky turned colors. Others continued to join us, dancing, hugging, singing, and looking upward with outstretched arms at the color-and-light show displayed in the heavens. It was a joyous culmination to a great day.

Suddenly, in the middle of our worship circle, a man beside me fell to the ground in an epileptic seizure. Mark from the Jesus Kitchen knelt down by his head, and two other men knelt on either side of him. I was at his legs, which were twitching violently as he convulsed. I reached out my hands over him and spoke the word God gave me, "Shalom," over him. The seizure instantly stopped and he lay there at peace. He was so suddenly still that one of the musicians stopped playing, wondering if he had died. I motioned for them to continue, figuring that worship in the Presence of God was exactly what we needed now. As I knelt down by him to find out how he was, he asked that the music and worship continue, as it was bringing him great peace. He said that he wasn't experiencing any of the pain or cramping he usually felt in his muscles after a seizure. I asked him if he wanted to sit up, and as he did he found himself sitting cross-legged on the ground; he began to look strangely at his legs and knees, placing his hands on them and shaking his head.

"My knees won't bend like this; I can't sit this way," he said slowly. We helped him up and he began to walk around, first very slowly, and then faster, exclaiming, "I'm not limping, I'M NOT LIMPING!" He repeated it louder and louder as he began to move faster and faster back and forth across the grass. "God healed my knees! There's no more pain! I'm healed!" he shouted.

I asked him what had happened, and he told me he was feeling no pain in his body for the first time in 26 years. He reached down to show me where the steel pins were in his knees, and he couldn't feel them. He probed, but they were gone! He was ecstatic.

It was growing darker, and just then the flash of someone's camera went off. The healed man, whose name is John, looked at me with a plan brewing in his mind and ran off in the direction of the flash. I looked over to see him standing directly in front of the camera and I saw the flash go off in his face. John ran back to me.

"Nothing happened! Whenever a bright flash goes off it triggers another seizure, but nothing happened!" He was so excited he wanted everyone to know. A crowd was gathering and the music was interrupted, so we had John pray for people who had knee problems, while my friend Jason asked who had back problems, and I had a "word of knowledge" from the Holy Spirit that God was healing headaches. A woman with a migraine came up to me and I barely touched her head when she shouted out: "It's gone!" I then had her pray for the people who were lining up behind her who also had headaches. Jason watched a young man's leg grow out almost an inch, which took care of his back pain. Backs, knees, and headaches were suddenly being healed, and while John was praying for knees he heard a "word of knowledge" for the first time in his life.

"Someone has a broken toe," he exclaimed.

"I broke my big toe," shouted one man. John prayed for him and God healed it! So many people were getting healed that there were clusters of healing groups, and many people heard the Holy Spirit give them words of prophetic encouragement and destiny for others. As they shared these, people began to feel a stronger and stronger Presence of God fill the meadow. Many just lay in the grass and had encounters with God; some were laughing and others were silent. A few couldn't get up for hours, and one had to be carried back to our camp much later by his friends; though he's been a believer for a long time, he said he had never "felt" God's Presence like that or been "drunk with the Holy Spirit." He stayed on the ground in our camp for hours, laughing, calling out, and speaking in tongues. His life was radically changed after that, and the journey he is on now would make a great story of its own.

In the midst of all the commotion, John came running up to me and shouted, "I have knuckles!" He held them up in front of my face and showed me, saying that before he could only hold his hands with his fingers straight out, as his knuckles had been crushed in an accident years ago. Previously he could only hold a glass of water with both hands, as the knuckles wouldn't bend. Now he had complete motion; God had given him new knuckles! He brought a friend over who confirmed his former condition to me. Heaven was breaking out all over the place.

While I headed back to the Bread of Life Kitchen, many people remained lying in the grass looking up at the stars and experiencing God, while Jason and Weston, a young man whose leg had grown out and whose back had been healed, wandered out among the camps with a few other friends. As he approached a kitchen at the edge of the meadow, Jason exclaimed: "God's healing people in the main meadow tonight. Does anyone have back pain?" One man had scoliosis and a short leg. The group prayed and his body and back straightened. Then he reached back and felt new muscle in his right shoulder where there had not been any, and he showed everyone where God had created the new muscle. The man with scoliosis could not bend down before, and now he could. Weston asked if he could pick up heavy things, and he said no. "Can you now?" He did. "Can you pick me up?" And he carried Weston around without pain, but with great laughter and joy.

Back at our camp healing revival broke out and went on into the night. Around the campfire people began praying for each other and many more legs grew out, while scoliosis, poor posture and balance, and stiffness in necks and shoulders were all healed. A right ear that was mostly deaf opened up and hearing was restored. Arches were created in one person's feet.

Later Jason led 30 to 50 people around the campfire into an encounter with Jesus, many of whom were not previously believers in Him. I then asked any who wanted to share to tell us what Jesus had said to them or shown them or given them. It was absolutely thrilling to hear the recounting of people's adventures and the truly amazing things they had heard and seen in the brief period of a 20-minute encounter with the Living God.

Two people lay on the ground for hours, overtaken by the Holy Spirit, and had amazing encounters of joy, revelation, and manifestations of speaking in tongues, shaking, and ecstasy. One man remained laughing and weeping until 4:30 in the morning. Many people experienced the glory of God and gave Him thanks and praise for His incredible Goodness toward all mankind.

The next morning a woman who came for breakfast told us that she had been in pain and her stomach had been bloated and protruding, but the night before she was completely healed at our campfire. John returned daily, and on the third day told us that after he'd been healed he had stopped taking the pain medication he'd been on for 26 years, and for the past three days had experienced no withdrawal. He said he had experienced a stomach healing once before after drinking from a river and had given credit for his healing to "the river," but now he knew that it is Jesus Christ who heals. "Jesus is my Healer; He's the One!" Many who encountered Him as their Healer were able to meet Him as their King, as His great Goodness showed them real evidence of His mercy and love. *Thank You, Jesus!*

Chapter Eight

AUTHORITY OVER THE WEATHER

ARIZONA NATIONAL RAINBOW GATHERING

We'd met other people at Rainbow Gatherings who knew Jesus, but since we had started attending as a kitchen in 1992 we had not seen another Christian camp. Finally in 1995 near Taos, New Mexico, a group from Minneapolis set up a small camp called the Jesus Kitchen near the main meadow. We were so excited when we heard about them that we gathered food, coffee, and anything we could find and made a procession down to their camp to greet them. They seemed a little shell-shocked and overwhelmed, but we welcomed them and prayed blessings and favor on them and treated them like family. Over the years we fell completely in love with them and even visited them in Minneapolis on our way to the Michigan Gathering.

Then in 1998 in Arizona two other new camps of Jesus freaks joined the gathering! We sent ambassadors to all three groups to welcome and embrace them with the love that we felt streaming from God's heart toward all of us. There's something about being in a culture that is different from your own that can make you feel you are alone. There's also something that the church sometimes emanates that can make you feel judged and that you are not welcome, not quite good enough, and maybe even in competition. We wanted to eliminate that negativity. It took a little work; Jody and I made several trips.

While walking through the main meadow on one of those trips, I noticed the large mural-like map of the gathering that someone paints each year to help people find all the varied camps spread out over about five square miles of forest. In the center of the map was a large heart signifying the main circle in main meadow. Dispersed among the camps were the four camps of Christian believers. I couldn't help but notice that they were laid out in four directions from main circle making the four points of a cross placed over the heart of the gathering. God orchestrated that! He loves the Rainbow tribes.

It was an extremely dry year and there was a fire ban in effect in the national forest. The Forest Service allowed kitchens to have cooking fires, but that was it. It was dusty and the forest was a tinderbox. Everyone was praying for rain. People sang for rain, drummed for rain, danced for rain, and did whatever their spiritual bent indicated for them to do. We decided to have the first-ever gathering of the Christian tribes and pray, celebrate, declare, and release the rain. Our friends came over from the four camps and we sang and danced to the music of drums and guitars as we worshipped and praised the Designer of rain. "Let it rain ... let it rain ..." One First Nations brother, a large and powerful man named Nelson, danced with all his might before the Lord. He had leather bands covered with large bells around his ankles and released such freedom as he danced and chanted that Heaven was rocked and I'm sure the angels joined in. He's since crossed over to that side, and I believe he's dancing with the angels over there. That day God knit our hearts together as different clans of one family and we all fell in love. We did a love-fire tunnel, which consisted of two lines of revelers facing each other. As others danced through the tunnel, we touched, blessed, prayed, and prophesied over them. Then they would be added to the end of the tunnel and those at the beginning would go through, creating a continuous tunnel of blessings. New people could enter at any time. Soon we found ourselves dancing in a downpour of rain! The forest floor turned from dust to mud, and everyone was elated. The drought was broken! And a turning point came for us as we initiated an annual event of holding at least one corporate assembling of all Christians at the gathering to come together for one night to worship and praise the Living God. In later years this would take place right in the main meadow.

COMMANDING THE STORM IN CALIFORNIA

Because we live outside for two weeks, we've had many experiences with influencing the weather at Rainbow Gatherings. A memorable one was in the Modoc National Forest in 2004. Morning meetings were becoming major events in which the Holy Spirit moved in many ways. One morning about 75 of us were sitting in a circle out in the open sunlight in a small meadow by the camp, capitalizing on the warmth of the mountain morning. We'd experienced a powerful time of worship, with drums and guitars and dancing and singing. I was teaching and leading an animated discussion on life in the Kingdom of God. In the west there suddenly appeared huge black thunderclouds moving at an ominous speed toward us, and we could see the rain already falling in the distance. Some looked around and several suggested running to the shelter of the worship tent, which was a huge canopy stretched out over a long crescent-shaped firepit near the kitchen. We were so focused together, and the Holy Spirit was downloading such awesome truth, that I felt to pick up and move at this moment would initiate a scattering that would cause us to lose our momentum and corporate revelation. The worship tent at this hour of the morning was partly filled with late-night carousers who had wandered into our camp around dawn and were wrapped in sleeping bags like cocoons around the warm ashes of the fire. These were interspersed with late-breakfast eaters and those who were passing through camp and not interested in being part of our meeting, or were listening from a safe distance. I just didn't want to move in on that space right then. I felt I caught a glimpse of the heart of God for that moment.

"Jesus said that when two or three of us are gathered in His Name He is here in the midst of us, right?" And when a consensus agreed, I added, "And that if two of us agree concerning anything we ask, it will be done for us by the Father." Agreed. "So turn around and look at that huge black cloud rolling toward us and let's command it to part in the middle and go around us."

Those who had been sitting with their backs to it now turned around and looked with shock at the threatening darkness roiling down upon us. We all began to command it to part and watched in wonder as the storm split and the wind blew and it passed around us leaving us under open skies as rain hit the forest on either side. It actually turned out to be a perfect illustration of our talk on the Kingdom of God and the authority we have in Christ. We'd been discussing the revelations we have of our position as sons and daughters and the promises and authority we have from that position, and how the opposition arises in this world toward us as we walk in the fullness of all of God's promises to us.

> *"... those who receive abundance of grace*
> *and the gift of righteousness will*
> *reign in life through the One, Jesus Christ."*
> *Romans 5:17*

CLIMBING MOUNT SNEFFELS

It was a glorious summer day in Telluride, a small mountain town nestled at 8,750 feet in a box canyon surrounded on three sides by 10,000- to 13,000-foot peaks. Linda and I lived there for ten and a half years, leading a family of believers and teaching a small group of adventurous young people how to walk in the Spirit. A dozen of us were planning a Jeep trip over Imogene Pass into Yankee Boy Basin to the base of Mount Sneffels. From there our goal was to climb the 14,150-foot peak by midday and then drive down to Ouray to soak in the hot springs, topping it off with a restaurant dinner to celebrate. Since there are always summer rain showers in the afternoon there, we gathered to ask God if this was what we were supposed to do that day. Part of our learning experience was to hear what God says and to go after it confidently, unhindered by circumstances. Several heard words of affirmation, and we all felt a peace in our spirits, which we took as confirmation, as we were learning to be led by His Peace in all things.

The drive upward through the San Juan Mountains was beautiful, and we stopped to explore in the turn-of-the-century ghost town of Tomboy near the old Tomboy Mine. After a photo shoot at the pass, we descended into a riot of wildflowers that covered the slopes for miles, past waterfalls, and then back up the climb toward the base of the mountain.

There were half a dozen cars at the trailhead when we arrived. But the main concern became the large bank of clouds moving in from all sides. Weather changes fast in the mountains; often you can experience three to four seasons in a day! We prayed and then scampered across the massive boulder fields that cover the lower slopes. The sky grew darker. We actually saw lightning flashing on the surrounding peaks. As we reached the steep rock-slide area we would use for our ascent, we saw groups of people hurrying down from the mountain as rain began to fall. The day became a cycle of wind, rain, and black clouds. Climbers scurried down the rocks and shouted out to us not to go up. A fellow I knew came over to severely warn us that we could die on the mountain. Turn back! The lightning flashed as thunder ripped the sky.

We decided to regroup in the semi-shelter of some gigantic rocks. Some in our party who had never climbed a mountain before were a little scared, and the most challenging section lay just ahead. As we donned rain gear, we asked for a consensus. Anyone could go back and wait in the vehicles, but several of us felt God *had* spoken to us and that we were to proceed and exercise authority and take the mountain. It sounded reasonable, if you weren't looking at the circumstances. One sister decided to stay behind, but she was particularly concerned for the first-timers. We chose to pray again and let each one make up his or her own mind. Our reasoning went something like this: "If God said we could climb the mountain, then the circumstance will just have to change; the weather will clear up as we stand together in agreement." I liked that. "Do we have Peace?" We embraced it and felt led by His Peace. So we rebuked the storm.

As we stepped back out into the wind, we expected victory over the weather to manifest and the day to turn abruptly. It didn't happen. It actually got worse! As we climbed, the wind picked up and it started *hailing!* Greg and I were leading the expedition, and we looked at each other and laughed. Opposition! We began to praise God loudly as we continued to climb the extremely steep ascent. The others followed. By the time we were almost to the saddle between the peaks, the rain and hail had stopped. When we reached the saddle we could see the storm hitting all the peaks around, complete with lightning shows, but it was actually clearing up above us! It was still a rough climb, and the air was thin and breathing was hard. We climbed a couloir, a steep narrow gulley filled with crunchy snow, before making the rugged boulder climb to the top. As the first of us reached the summit, there were actually holes in the grey sky where sun streamers poked through. It turned out that a couple of our first climbers were afraid of heights and they had settled onto a lower ledge with a secure back rest, so we sent a party down to nurture them to the top, and we surrounded them so they didn't feel so exposed to the steep drop that plummeted on every side. Then as we ate lunch the sun appeared, though the storm still raged on the surrounding peaks! We cheered and praised the God who is greater than all of our circumstances.

The hike down was great fun — skiing down the couloir, having snowball fights, and feeling the thrill of victory. When we got to the saddle, three of us ran and leaped off, hitting the ridiculously steep gravel slide with the aid of gravity and ski-sliding down it at a deadly rate. I held two rocks in my hands and used them to balance side-to-side as I sped downward with one foot under my butt and the other out in front to steer me, and I remember thinking: "What am I doing?!!" Racing down at full speed, we had to dodge boulders that could have launched us airborne to die an untimely death, splattered on the rocks below. Ah, the thrill of adrenaline! Needless to say, the others didn't follow suit but climbed down in a more sensible manner. But we all received a lesson in the faithfulness of God to see us through when He says, "Go," despite all circumstances and evidence to the contrary. We need to know that He is trustworthy.

OUTDOOR WEDDINGS

A significant number of people in our community were in their twenties, a particularly ripe age for courtship and marriage, so I performed quite a few weddings during my time in Telluride. Living in the midst of such beautiful surroundings made outdoor weddings very popular. But since storms materialize every afternoon in the summer-time, the weather is always an issue in the mountains.

I was teaching the students in the School of the Spirit about the authority we have in Christ, about the open Heaven we live in, about what Christ did for us when he died on the cross, about the finished work that brings us into a place of favor with God as sons and daughters, and about the Holy Spirit who empowers us to do the works that He did ... and even greater works. Some of these searching young people came from church backgrounds that had experienced little if any healing. They'd adopted a theology of experience that taught them that sometimes God healed people and sometimes He didn't because perhaps it wasn't his will for that person. We had to hack down some pretty thick, choking vines of unbelief in order to begin to sow seeds of truth and faith.

So that's when we started teaching these students to believe God to change the weather. They hadn't had any previous doctrinal instruction that specifically opposed the idea, and most of them had never even thought about it. Plus, Jesus had done it. Our many hikes, campouts, worship celebrations in the park, and weddings offered plenty of opportunities to practice changing the weather. And each time we would experience the successful results of our experiments, our faith would grow.

It got so that we'd be gathering for an outdoor wedding and the dark clouds would loom ominously as if they were gathering with us. Someone would always ask the question, "Do you think we need to move this inside?" I'd look around for one of my people and smile at him or her, and I'd catch a mischievous grin in return. Then I'd call out to everyone, believers and unbelievers alike, offering all an opportunity to see the goodness of God.

"Who wants to help change the weather?" A few of my School of the Spirit students would always respond, as well as an interesting array of cousins, friends of the groom, and party drunks. Then I'd ask if we were all in agreement, and when we had consensus that we were, I'd tell them, "Now we're all going to turn toward those clouds and tell them to leave, and call the sun to come out and shine." I loved to see the thrill that complete strangers would take in joining in, and the gratification that would come only minutes later. We'd spend the rest of the afternoon like we were old friends who had been through something profound together.

Some of the parents of our students had great difficulty accepting the idea that we could actually have authority over the weather. They knew we were abnormal and already had a lot of questions for us. And though they couldn't refute that Jesus had done it in the bible, they would ask us:

"But why *weather*?"

"Because it's *easy*," I'd reply. "No doctrines or sacred cows, no 'Aunt Martha loved the Lord and prayed and didn't get healed.' Or rather, no 'Uncle Leroy tried to change the weather and it didn't work and he got struck by lightning instead!' You don't have those kinds of stories, so it's easy!" They still thought we were abnormal, but they did become more curious.

One family's change in particular was a real joy to witness. Their son was growing and changing and they wanted some of what he had, so they started attending our bible studies. Their background had been pretty traditional, but they were very open to learning.

Their son's wedding was set to take place in the mountains, so it was great fun for us to anticipate changing the weather, since the father was still skeptical about it all. And this wedding wasn't simply an outdoor wedding, it was an entire weekend-campout celebration. It was wonderful. After a worship jam and sharing time on Sunday morning, we broke up to get dressed for the big event in the early afternoon.

Sure enough, the clouds rolled in. It was looking very grey, and even though it wasn't raining yet, it wasn't very cheery weather for a wedding. So I popped the question: "Who wants to change the weather?" I got a good response, and after a few minutes even the groom's dad decided to join in. Excellent.

"How long do you think it will work for?" he asked.

"How about if you pick a time? Choose the exact hour you want the rain to fall," I replied.

"Four o'clock," was his choice. This made it so much more exciting.

The wedding was beautiful and the sun came out right on cue; afterwards we had a feast and visited old and new friends, folks distant and near. By three o'clock we were cleaning up, with everyone breaking camp and packing out. We arrived at the trucks and had just finished stuffing the last items in and tying them all down when the first raindrops hit. We all checked our watches — four o'clock, straight up. The dad was ecstatic! He's something of a competitor and really likes to win, and this was quite an accomplishment for him. High fives all around! I looked at him as I hopped into the truck, and he was grinning from ear to ear. *Thanks especially for that one!*

201

GLORY ~ MANY NATIONS, ONE VOICE

Telluride is one of the most amazing places to live. With a population of about 2,000, it is small enough for people to walk almost everywhere. There is world-class skiing right in the back yard in the winter, and in the summertime the San Juan Mountains offer the most spectacular setting to be found for hiking, backpacking, climbing, and four-wheeling. The pristine lakes and rivers are prime for fishing and, during high water, for kayaking and rafting. It's a wonderland. From June through September there are festivals every weekend — music, art, drama, and film festivals that draw crowds from all over the nation.

A beautiful town park surrounded by mountain peaks and waterfalls serves as the setting for many festivals and sporting events. The park calendar is always so full that I used to go to the parks office in February to secure two dates in the summer — two Sunday mornings when we could enjoy "Church in the Park" to celebrate Jesus in the midst of this awe-inspiring setting. With some juggling and a whole lot of favor, I could usually get a date in July and one in August. We'd put together a band made up of friends from all over, jam all Saturday night, and be ready Sunday morning to rock the park with a great worship experience. Then we'd preach and pray, sometimes perform some skits, and finish off with an open barbecue and pot-luck feast. I loved "Church in the Park." People rode their bikes through, young mothers pushing baby strollers stopped to listen, baseball and soccer games happened all around us, and the music played over and through it all. Folks in the mountains who heard the music would hike down from Bear Creek to see what was happening. Without walls or ceiling, it felt as if we were mingling with all of humanity. The town cops and the homeless would come by and share lunch with us; vacationers traveling through town would join us in worship. It was alive and free, and we had the opportunity to love and minister to a wide variety of people. Fun and spontaneous things would happen each time. I loved it.

It was also a perfect opportunity to play around with the weather. There were so many occasions of week-long rainy spells that were broken on Sunday mornings as we prayed and declared open heavens and clear skies. It was always great fun to pick the exact time when the rain could fall, always allowing ourselves enough time to clean up and haul all our equipment back and unload it in the safety of the building. Then we'd look at the clock and celebrate God's goodness as the summer rain would rattle the windows at precisely the stated time. It may sound arrogant, but we know that it is only our relationship with God and "Christ in us" that allows us to have such authority. I feel that we honor God by radically exercising our faith to do the impossible, and that He delights in us as a Good Father when He sees His children take on a challenge with passion and joy. Holy Spirit really likes to have fun with us.

One summer, some musician friends from Florida stayed with us. They had a sound system that kicked us into a whole new dimension and had the neighbors asking what was happening. Although it was great fun, I did have to do a little follow-up with explanations and apologies. Those same friends started to talk about having a worship festival in the town park. "Let's burst open the Heavens and declare the praises of God over this whole region." It sounded good; we decided to go for it.

Festivals are done with excellence in Telluride, and we were schooled in the fine art of protocol and diplomacy all the next winter as Greg and I took on all of the home-front work, while our friends Marlo and Aaron set things up from afar as they traveled and put on conferences. We attended countless meetings, applied to several boards for different levels of approval, signed contracts and made up plans, followed required guidelines, met monthly deadlines, and acted as if we were administrators, which we are definitely not. We recruited helpers and found some great talent in the family. We had people help with creating artwork, setting up, tearing down, advertising, preparing food, providing supplies and transportation, making phone calls, canvassing all of Western Colorado, housing the performers, providing meals, and doing countless other things. I could write an entire book on the experience, but the thing I want to talk mostly about is the *weather*.

We'd planned for a three-day, multi-cultural experience from Friday through Sunday, with the main event being a series of worship concerts all day Sunday. Our headliners were a black gospel band from the inner city, a group of drummers from six African nations, a Latino rhythm band, a Native American group consisting of a dozen First Nations people in full regalia called 120 Drums of Thunder, and a lively Celtic band. Hence the name: Glory ~ Many Nations, One Voice. As we developed the plan in greater detail, it consisted of declaring the goodness of Creator God and praising Him in the midst of His creation through the vehicle of varied cultural musical and dance forms. Worshippers and intercessors from all over the Western Slope of Colorado wanted to join us as we proclaimed and honored the Living God in one of the high places of Colorado. So much time, money, and energy are spent in these mountains lifting up the pleasures of music, art, nature, sports, and just plain having fun, so we wanted to pour our time, money, and energy into headlining and thanking the God who placed us here and loves us as we pursue all of these adventures. We wanted to connect the goodness of Heaven with our position on earth and watch what happens when we thank Him and give Him glory.

As the event drew near, problems and various forms of opposition arose. First, the parks department decided to re-sod the grass in the area we were scheduled to use. But the re-sodded grass wasn't growing because of drainage problems, so the sodding had to be redone and it had to be leveled; no one knew if it would be ready in time. We went to the park and prayed over the grass and it grew back beautifully. But then our summer monsoon season began. The resulting problem was that the now-thick grass had become a spongy wet bog that wouldn't dry out. We started declaring sunshine and told the parks staff we were praying. They were wonderful to work with, and when the sun peeked out the Monday before the festival they were excited and told us to keep it up. Things were looking good, until we found that a sprinkler had been left on or broken, and the field was flooded. Then on Tuesday the rains returned.

Marlo and his crew pulled in under grey skies with a semi-load of sound equipment and a whole team of roadies, musicians, and sound men. Friends, intercessors, workers, and the bands began to arrive from all over the country, and we ended up with a crew of around 100 people to put on the event. Energy was mounting, and it felt like a beehive all around the church building. We had turned the sanctuary into a dining room to feed everyone, and Linda headed up a staff of phenomenal cooks and prep cooks to put out the meals. She also had her team chopping buckets full of vegetables and meat in preparation for the feast on Sunday: our famous elk-steak fajitas for over 400 people and around 200 portabella-mushroom fajitas for the vegetarians, with a side of tabouli and Western Slope peaches for dessert.

In a resort town the profit margin is always a huge consideration, so we decided to be of the opposite spirit and *give* an amazing experience and an excellent meal for free to all. I believe we spent over $40,000, a lot of which came from donations.

On Friday it was still raining, but we prayed and it stopped long enough for us to proceed with our parade down Main Street. The Native Americans in full regalia were out in front, and at every intersection they would stop and perform a native dance that drew a crowd and impressed us all. A group of us followed in wild array — men wearing African outfits and women in colorful dresses, some of us blowing shofars and conch shells and anything that made noise. The Africans followed, not to be outdone by the First Nations people; as they reached the intersections, they stopped and set up a drum circle and let it rip. People were streaming out of the shops and restaurants to see what was happening. The Latinos had a percussion band going and followed the Africans, and so on. The overall feeling was of an outlandish and explosive *Celebration of Joy* pouring through town like a river, complete with a powerful tribal soundtrack. By the time we arrived at the little park on Main Street right by the Farmers' Market, the Africans and the Latinos had a full-on drum circle going that drew a crowd of dancers. The Native Americans took the stage and shared from their hearts, and then a group of teens did a few choreographed numbers mixing drama and dance with music. It was a great hit. It started to rain right before the end, and we all headed to the church for a celebration dinner and time of prayer, praise, and worship. Over 100 of us were packed like sardines around the tables that filled every inch of the room, and the serving counters groaned under the bounty of the feast. It was a time of connecting with old friends and new, and celebrating the goodness of God until late into the night. Saturday it poured again. Someone brought the news that it was scheduled to rain all weekend.

We'd prepared some events to take place outside on Saturday, which necessitated good weather. These events were canceled, but there was still plenty of prep work to do indoors, so a large crew kept working throughout the day in the building while a group of men built the stage under the canvas canopy in Town Park. As it turned out, we really needed this time to prepare for the enormous event the next day.

As we were working on the stage in the rain and looking over the soaking wet, soupy field in front of it that was our dancing and seating area, a debate arose about what we should do. Our Telluride crew consisted of School of the Spirit students and folks from our church family. We'd prayed and declared for months that we'd have a clear day, and we brooded over this section of the park like a mother hen over her eggs. Several of us had already seen clear skies in the heavenly unseen realms and some of us had simply believed it. Our more professional out-of-town friends, however, with their years of experience in production, had the entire sound system and all the logistics of its set-up to think about. In the natural it just didn't make sense to continue our preparations as if it weren't going to continue to rain.

The Town Park staff had generously offered us the much larger, semi-enclosed and covered stage across the park, where the ground drained well and the grass would be drier. This is where the larger music festivals were held which seated 12,000 people. We were looking at a maximum of only 1,000 people, which would be dwarfed in the larger field. There were so many factors to be looked at that I knew I could only go with how I felt the Lord was leading us. When we'd prayed, seen, and dreamed it, the festival had been on this smaller field. When I prayed, I had peace. When we discussed options, I felt unrest.

Our out-of-town friends suggested taking a final walk over to the larger main stage to make a decision before proceeding further. They had a lot of doubts and concerns, which was understandable. As they headed off, I sat on the smaller stage watching the rain and listening. *God, You've never let us down yet. I know You're going to pull this off. But a break in the rain right now would really help.* One of our young men from School of the Spirit came over to me with a concerned look on his face. "You always teach us about faith and opposition. You're not going to give in, are you?" he asked with what sounded like a hint of disillusionment. A huge machine was in motion and a lot was at stake.

"I feel like they need to hear for themselves, so we can be in unity. I'm praying for God to speak clearly to them as well. Thanks, buddy, for your support and concern." And we hopped up together and followed the others across the park to the main stage. After much pacing, talking, thinking, praying, Marlo asked me what I thought. I pointed my thumb over toward the little stage under the white canopy that looked like a couple of tipis in the distance and smiled. We finally came to a consensus to use the original location and headed back across the wet fields in the rain to finish the drum platform and set up the sound tent. As it was getting dark, a large part of our crew went back to Mission Control Center at the church to dry off and get ready for dinner.

I'd imagined that our new unity would bring all the circumstances into proper order and the sky would clear up and the field would have a night to dry out. Instead, the sky ripped open and the wind blew harder, and we had a difficult time just keeping the tent from blowing away as we held on like sailors in gale-force winds trying to tie ropes to rebar stakes in the ground and getting completely drenched. A call came for us to abandon ship and join the family for a warm, dry dinner celebration, but a few of us stayed in the cold, wet darkness and secured things for the night. We decided to choose laughter and joy in the soaking-wet face of opposition.

When we returned to the dining hall, the place was packed and glowing with a golden light and resounding with the din of over a hundred partying feasters. Steam rose off our clothes and our hair dripped in our faces as smiling friends offered us plates of hot food. Newly arrived shipping crates containing 120 hand drums filled every available spot in the already crowded foyer and along the west wall of the over-stuffed great room, vying for space with sound equipment and tons of assorted personal luggage. The feeling of friends and family and feasting and home-for-the-holidays celebrating pervaded, yet it somehow mixed with the feeling of travelers being stuck in a train depot overnight during a hurricane. After we sang and prayed and declared clear weather for the next morning, the tables were pushed back and bedding was laid out in patchwork array all over the carpet. No one really knew what tomorrow might bring, and all we had to go with was His Presence, but His Presence is *really good*.

A black family from Denver that none of us knew had arrived and needed a place to stay for the night. It was curious, because Greg and I had tried to secure an inner-city black gospel band to open the event, but without success. It turned out that this family was part of a church singing group, and after a five-minute audition the next morning we signed them up.

Sunday morning dawned bringing the clearest skies we had seen in a month! Overhead was the deep Colorado blue that is seen only in the thin air at high altitude and almost takes the breath away. The sun was pouring forth warmth, and we could feel God smiling over us.

Only four hours remained to complete the set-up in the park, and the hyper-bustling began. Marlo and his crew were outstanding to watch as they pulled out the contents of a semi-trailer and turned it into a functioning festival stage, sound system, and control board complete with sound checks, all ready by ten o'clock! The rest of us set up eight ten-by-ten-foot white e-z-up tents along the west and south perimeters of the partially drying, hockey-rink-sized oval grass field that was to be our festival seating area. Three of these tent canopies were joined into an L-shape to become our outdoor kitchen, and tables, propane stoves, and giant woks were brought in and an efficient functioning cooking scene appeared before our eyes, being put into operation even as it was still manifesting. Our prophetic "Divine Guidance" Tent shared the hill on the south side with the Healing Tent. About twenty 16-foot aluminum conduit flagpoles were impaled into the wet ground around the perimeter of the oval and topped with colorful silken streamers that flapped in the light breeze, giving it the look of a renaissance fair.

Sound checks and music began to fill the air as porta-potties were dropped off and the Town Park staff stopped by to look over the set-up and offer encouragement and help. They were wonderfully affirming. Parking-attendant volunteers were directing traffic and folks were beginning to stream into the park. The majority of the grassy area was surprisingly dry, but there was still a boggy section that extended about 20 feet from the front of the stage. Some of us danced in it, but most of the people set up lawn chairs and blankets quite a way back as the sound booming from the stage was impressive. So much was happening as I ran around checking off a note-pad-long list of to-do items, that I was surprised to suddenly hear the singing-preaching-hollering-testifying of the gospel group take over and realized that the event had actually begun; we were fully underway.

I looked at my watch; it was 10:30, and I was blown away that we'd actually pulled it off! There is a certain thrill that comes with seeing how much is accomplished when a huge team tackles a job and each individual does the part he or she was created for, using all the gifting and skill and joy that is within. I looked over the vast setting and saw details that no one but the small crew who had crafted them knew about, but each of those details now added to the excellence and beauty of the whole event. It was stunning.

Many townspeople were drawn to the park by the first blue-sky Sunday in a month; others were drawn to the music, and some turned up specifically to see the African and First Nations drummers. And there were lots of visitors from the neighboring Western Slope towns. We were especially thrilled to see folks who had come from the nearby Southern Ute Reservation. Dancing to the African drummers was the morning highlight for many, and an outpouring of explosive joy swept through the park as the fullness of joy that permeates Heaven filled the earth.

Native people are steeped in an honoring protocol, and when the First Nations group hit the stage it was as if a power bomb had been dropped. They honored Greg and me with tribal shirts and necklaces over which they spoke prophetic meaning. I honored them by presenting them with two glass quart jars, one containing water from the San Miguel River that flows through town, and one containing soil from the earth under us. I honored them as the ones God had set as first stewards of this land and asked their forgiveness for building on their land without asking their permission, on behalf of both the church and the town. That statement and a photo made the front page of the local newspaper, *The Daily Planet*, the next day. Then we all honored God as the Creator of all, Father of all people, and Jesus as King of Heaven's Kingdom, Lord and Savior of all people. They broke into songs and dances to the drums as they thanked God for His goodness and asked Him to continue to bless this earth. As we honored God with the First Nations people, and honored them as first stewards of the earth in this region by God's design, they in turn conferred an authority upon us as the *church* of God, representatives of His Kingdom here on earth, and delegated to us authority over the atmosphere of this region. The experience was powerful.

We broke for lunch, and Linda and her crew blessed everyone with an outrageous meal. The elk steaks had been marinating in a thick sauce for over a day and the fajitas were off the charts. People raved. The sun stayed strong in the sky. People marveled.

After the meal, the Native Americans handed out the 120 hand drums to the assembly of people. A scripture verse had been written on each drum, and the speaker explained that as we drummed we were releasing the truth of those scriptures into the atmosphere. And then they led out, carrying the rhythm on the large floor drum that four of them stood around and beat upon. We all responded in unison on our 120 hand drums. It was an epochal experience. As we continued, there came a time when we all beat in unison, led by the First Nations people, releasing Heaven's truths into the atmosphere, and then for a moment we stopped. Suddenly there was a crack from the Heavens like thunder and many of us looked around; I saw the sound men looking puzzled and trying to figure out where it came from. We continued the drumbeats, building momentum, and when we paused again, there was the responding thunder crack. The sky was still bright blue with no thunderclouds in sight. We were astonished. There's something about the unity of mankind's tribes when they come together to honor and love God and each other that causes Heaven to get involved!

There's also something about the energy of local and regional forces that are established in an area and familiar to it. They become entrenched and resistant to a Heavenly takeover of love and mercy and honor and generosity and Truth. But when we His people press in and daily grow more persistent against all opposition, persevering in love and mercy and honor and generosity and Truth, we see Heaven break out and overcome the temporal circumstances of this earth. Then God displays His eternal victory and unlimited power and abundance and we enter into it and get to participate in it. Even the weather changes!

Chapter Nine

SOME ADVENTURES INTO THE UNSEEN REALMS

THIN PLACES

Many of the adventures we have in the miraculous take us into those places where the heavenly realms and the earthly physical world come so close together. That is when the very air around us is charged with the atmosphere of Heaven, and our earthly situations, circumstances, health, weather, and even economy are affected by Heaven's economy. Sometimes we can feel the separation between the two realms becoming very thin, and in those *thin places* it's often easy to see into the unseen realms, or even to slip over into them altogether.

THE THRONE ROOM

One morning I was worshipping the Lord on my

knees with my face bowed to the ground. I was experiencing His Presence so strongly, when suddenly my surroundings vanished and Heaven opened up all around me. I found myself before the Throne of God in all its Glory. I saw the beauty, the splendor, the glory, and the amazing colors that surrounded the Throne, as well as the Radiance of the One on the Throne. I felt a holy terror pass through me and I noticed I was trembling and shaking, and though I peeked, I dared not get up off my face.

Then Jesus stood up from the Throne and extended a sword toward me that shot out from His hand like a blue-white laser-beam of light, reminding me of a light saber from *Star Wars*. It reached me and touched me, and it was as if I were being knighted. I felt something awesome go through me, and I stayed in that state for a while, experiencing intense peace and pleasure.

Then I looked up at Jesus, and He had His head cocked to one side a little, with a funny grin on His face and a twinkle in His eye, looking almost mischievous. I slowly stood up and looked at Him. It was as if He were waiting for me to ask Him something, like He was saying: "Come on! I know you want it." I looked at the sword (I really like swords) and at Him, and asked: *"Can I try it?"* I was astonished and delighted as He held it out toward me! I took it and suddenly it was like a fire hose in my hands under full pressure, pulling me this way and that. He laughed and laughed as I struggled to control it, and I finally got it to settle down for me.

The scene shifted and I saw a group of black-shadow people stuck in a miry bog with a grey stringy glue-like substance pulling them down into the slime. Jesus said to me: "This works on such as these," pointing to the sword and then to the people stuck in the slime. I took the sword I had barely mastered and swung at one of the people to cut him free from the gluey stuff, but the sword was still a little unwieldy and it sliced right through his neck, looking like it had severed his head. "Aaarghh!" I freaked. I felt totally irresponsible using a weapon that was way out of my league.

Jesus said it was no problem, and as I looked more closely I saw the man stand up, completely whole and free and full of life and color! So I started hacking at the others, and though it looked at first like mutilation, each one emerged free and whole! Jesus was cheering me on as I did this, and as I returned to this realm, I felt as if He had given me a tool and a commission to do a work for Him. I'm still not sure how it will all play out, but I've experienced some victory and success with it and it's exciting to be a part of — *and* it's a really cool sword.

THE KING ON A HORSE

I was worshipping in a group of about 800 people and I was having a hard time connecting with God, which is unusual. After a while I asked: *"Where are You right now, Jesus?"* I began to try to imagine the Throne Room but it wasn't really happening, so I asked: *"You aren't always just on the Throne, are You?"*

All of a sudden my vision seemed to blur, and I saw before me a smoky cloud that burned away a large space right in front of me, leaving the smoking perimeter of a six-by-nine-foot rectangle standing upright before me. Through it Heaven burst into this realm, and I was

217

overwhelmed by a King on a white horse rearing up right in front of me, and I almost fell backwards at the impact of the vision. The horse was magnificent and so was the rider, dressed in white and gold with a golden crown on His Head and radiant in His Glory. The horse was powerful, rearing and snorting and turning this way and that, unable to stay in one place as if chomping at the bit to leap forward into a full gallop, restrained only by the power of the Rider. I thought to myself that He must be reining in this remarkable creature with great strength and skill, but when I looked I saw that there were no reins or bit at all. The absolute Peace of the King maintained control over the horse. This glorious King never lost composure at any time, and I marveled at the perfect peace that radiated from Him. All of a sudden I understood that this powerful horse was the *Ministry of the Kingdom*, ready to move in any direction with full force and strength the second the King moved the slightest muscle to nudge it that way. I was in awe. Suddenly the King said to me:

"Come up here!"

Fear and terror swept over me, and I looked up in wonder as the strangest thoughts went through my head. First I wondered where I would sit — in front? Behind? Then I wondered if I would be really tiny and He would be huge in comparison. As I was puzzling over this, the King reached down and took hold of me and pulled me up to Himself as He repeated a booming: "Come up here!" Suddenly I was seated on the horse, and *I was the King*, and I was *in the King* and *the King was in me* and we were *ONE!* It was the most extraordinary experience, and I suddenly knew His heart and mind and we resonated as one.

"This is how we'll do the ministry from now on," He said in the softest voice imaginable that created an incredible stillness inside me that then seemed to radiate all around me. It was wondrous.

I heard a distant: "It's time to transition ...," as someone was moving us from the time of worship into a teaching time. I blinked and looked around and found I was lying on the steps of the stage, kind of sprawled out, the band was finished, and the crowd of worshippers and dancers was moving from the area in front of the stage back into the auditorium seating. Someone reached out a hand to help me up, but it was really difficult to get back to my seat.

TRANSPORTED?

I was awakened in the middle of the night by the harsh ringing of the telephone. Stumbling across the room to find it, I answered, partly just to stop its clamor, and partly because I felt sure it must be our son, Jesse. He was in the army and had been stationed in Afghanistan for two separate tours of duty. He would call via satellite phone when he got the chance, which was almost always at some strange hour of the night. It just felt like it was one of his calls.

"Dad, where were you half an hour ago?" he asked, his voice exploding through the receiver and running at full throttle.

I squinted at the clock to see the time. "Jesse, I was right here in bed, sound asleep. It's two in the morning."

Still at full volume, speed, and dramatic intensity, he

raced on, "No, Dad, you were right *here!* I saw you."

"Okay, Jesse, tell me about it."

And the story unfolded. He told me he was being chased by terrifying, bat-like demonic monsters that were intent on killing him. "Dad, I wasn't drunk or on drugs; I wasn't dreaming. I was awake and they came after me. I was more scared than I've ever been in my life. I've been in battle and under fire, and I've never been this scared. They were going to kill me!" And he described the chase of these horrifying monsters as I listened in the dark of my bedroom. "And, Dad, as they came after me to kill me, I called out to *you*. And you appeared, and with a flaming sword you drove them away!"

"Wow, Jesse. I believe you. That's incredible, but I'm sure that's how it happened. How are you doing now?" And I prayed with him and brought the peace of God into the situation and we talked for a while and said goodnight and hung up. But I pondered the situation in my heart and asked God to let me remember when such things happen the next time.

"... UNUSUAL MIRACLES ..."

I'm fascinated by what God does and especially how He heals. I love it when He heals. The stories in this book are sprinkled with a few stories of healing, but I could write an entire book of outrageous healing miracles I've seen Him pull off in over 30 years. But one of the real thrills I experience is when I can *see* into the *unseen* realm — see what He is doing there and then watch it unfold in the natural or physical realm. Jesus said that He did only what He **saw** the Father do. The Apostle Paul tells us in his second letter to the Corinthians in chapter four, verse 18:

> *"... we do not **look at** the things which are **seen**,*
> *but at the things which are **unseen**.*
> *For the things which are **seen** are temporary,*
> *but the things which are **unseen** are eternal."*

And the writer of the book of Hebrews speaks of Moses:

> *"... he **looked to** the reward ... not fearing ...*
> *for he endured as **seeing** Him who is **invisible**."*
> *Hebrews 11:26,27*

"I want to be like You, Jesus." And like Paul and Moses. So I'll share just two stories of unusual miracles that entailed seeing into the unseen realm.

I met a young man who had been in a serious accident some years before and had broken both his elbows and injured his back. His entire body went through severe trauma, and while he had full casts on his elbows he found that his spine had begun to bend over and his rib cage was compressing at an alarming rate. As the compression increased steadily over time, his ribs began to put pressure on his organs, especially his heart and lungs. He told me that the doctors suggested breaking his ribs and resetting them to try to relieve the pressure that was making it hard for him to breathe. That sounded terrible. So I asked if I could pray for him.

He was very willing, and he closed his eyes as he stood before me, ready to receive. Instead of placing my hands on him and beginning to pray, I stepped back and *looked*. I saw a cylinder of light come down from Heaven and engulf him, so that he was completely immersed in the light. I felt a child-like curiosity urging me to touch the glowing substance that surrounded him. As I reached my hand through the light I decided to gently touch him in the middle of his back. I heard an explosive pop, pop, pop! Both of our eyes opened wide at the sound, and I asked him excitedly, "Did you *feel that?*" He replied affirmatively, as he stood up straight as an arrow with his chest expanded. "What *happened?*" He told me that his entire skeletal structure had shifted and changed shape in two seconds! "I can breathe deeply!" he exclaimed. That night he slept with unprecedented comfort and was full of joy and gratitude the next day. God had done a great work and I was supremely thankful to be a part of it.

The next miracle involved a woman who complained of intense pain in her ovaries and in her spine. I looked and saw a spear sticking out of her belly that went through her ovaries and lodged in her spine.

"Excuse me, but I see a spear extending out of your stomach that goes through your ovaries and is stuck in your spine. Would you mind if I pulled it out?" She looked at me a little quizzically and slowly shook her head indicating that no, she would not mind. I grabbed hold of the invisible spear and pulled it out. Instantly the woman cried out and raised her hands in the air. Suddenly she began to dance around with her arms still in the air, declaring that the pain was completely gone.

I suddenly knew in my spirit the source of her pain, and I spoke to her about it. "I believe there has been a curse spoken over you against childbearing, to rob you of your motherhood. Do you know about this?" She nodded her head. "Then let's break it off." I told her God had given her back her authority over her body, and she then gave her body back to Him and we declared every curse null and void, as Jesus had already taken the curse upon Himself when He died, which made her free. She thanked me and continued to dance around praising God, completely free of pain and oppression for the first time in over a year!

Chapter Ten

BROKERING HEAVEN

THE PROPHECIES

In the fall of 2008 Linda and I moved to Redding, California, to become part of Bethel Church and experience their School of Supernatural Ministry. At this time I received some extraordinary and random prophecies. Five times in one week people I didn't know told me I was going to release supernatural finances for the Kingdom of God. Another person even drew a picture for me of dollar signs falling from heaven and a bank on the earth. Another woman saw gold coins falling on me, and some of them were filled with chocolate inside! She said God was going to mix provision with joy and delight.

I've received many prophetic words, but only once do I remember a word about finances. I was fully willing to receive these words. So I began to pray and release this promise over everyone I knew who needed money, which is a lot of people in a school of supernatural ministry that sends out 1,200 students on ministry trips into more than

30 nations. And though I felt something was happening, I also felt sure that there was something more I was supposed to be doing. So I went to the Lord for a strategy.

I was in the Bethel prayer house soaking in the Spirit when I sensed a plan coming from God. I believe He told me to take ten $10 bills and give them to ten young women that He would highlight to me who needed their international trip fees paid. Then He wanted me to give them each a father's blessing and declare an opening up of channels of provision for them. The rest was up to Him.

Each young lady was touched and delighted, received the $10 bill with the blessing and prayer, and promised to tell me when their money came in. And all of them received the full amount needed for their trips.

That was exciting, and I kept seeing superb financial miracles happen in new and different ways. By the fall of 2009 I was aware of many more needs, both for school fees and ministry trips. So I stepped things up.

THE ENCOUNTER

I was at home one morning with an hour or so to spare, so I decided to lie on the couch and meet with God. It's one of my most favorite things to do. I was praising Him for His goodness when suddenly everything around me changed and I found myself in the Treasury Room of Heaven and Jesus was there with me. I knew where I was somehow, without being told, and I realized I was looking at an entire wall of gold bricks that seemed to go on for miles. I remember telling Jesus that I didn't know what I'd do with gold bricks, and asked if He had any cash. Thinking back on it, it sounds ridiculous. He motioned to me to turn around and I saw what looked like library shelves that went on forever. On the shelves were hundred-dollar bills bound together into thousand-dollar bundles and filling the never-ending shelves like books. I asked if I could have $10,000 to pay the school fees for three students I knew, and He said, "Sure." He handed me a wrinkled brown paper bag, which I thought was funny, since this was Heaven and all, and we filled it with wads of hundred-dollar bills. Then I came back to myself, lying on my couch in my living room, but the bag of money was nowhere to be seen.

I told a good friend about it, and he took three one-dollar bills out of his wife's purse and handed them to me saying, "Here's a start!" So I placed a green sticky note on each bill and wrote four zeros on the note with a black marker, and went looking for the three people.

"This looks like one dollar, but see, there are really four zeros at the end here. So I'm going to release the finances of Heaven over you and give you a father's blessing and swipe your ATM card on the Father's account in Heaven. Be blessed!"

The first person was jubilant; he fell back into the vending machine in the hallway and wiggled and jerked as he made it onto the floor howling. That seemed like "joy and delight" to me. The next two were amused and receptive. It was fun, but I wasn't really satisfied. The more we heard of people in need, the more Linda and I passed out $10 bills, often with the extra zeros attached, and I would pray a father's blessing, and people would be impacted and filled with joy.

One day we were in Advanced Ministry Training in

an Encounters Class where a woman who is famous for taking people on encounters in Heaven was ministering. At the end there was a question-and-answer time, so I popped the question: "How do you get things that Jesus has given you in Heaven into this realm?" Her answer was simple: "If I knew how to do that, I'd have tons of stuff." But she suggested doing a prophetic act, such as the ones I'd been doing in giving away $1 and $10 bills.

THE HOT TUB

One night in February of 2010, I was soaking in a hot tub with seven wild revivalist friends from three nations, and the Spirit of the Lord fell in a marvelous way. We were completely overwhelmed by His joy and Presence and found ourselves in exhilarated cycles of praising God, laughing, prophesying, laughing, and praying for hours. At one point a young man prophesied over me that God was calling me to be a "Broker of Heaven." It was a lengthy message, but in it the Lord said I had proven myself faithful and that He trusted me to "Broker the Finances of Heaven." He then repeated the word "Broker." It was late when we all crawled out of the hot tub and drove home under the influence of the Holy Spirit and tried to remember and then write down the powerful words of grace we'd received.

I meditated on the concept for several days, when I sensed the Lord leading me to look up the word "broker." I got out the gigantic volume of my dad's old *Oxford Dictionary of the English Language* and found this:

BROKER - *from a Middle English word BROACH*
- a sharp object used to tap a cask of wine, hence -

to broach or tap a cask; and an Anglo Saxon word BRUCAN - to use, possess, enjoy.
Definition: a tapster who retails wine; an agent or retail dealer; a person paid a fee or commission for acting as an agent in making contracts; a middleman generally; an interpreter, messenger, commissioner.

As a BROKER OF HEAVEN I get to tap the cask of New Wine and use, possess, and enjoy it, while acting as an agent in distributing Heaven's resources to others. I liked it! I decided it defined my new identity, and I would believe it, declare it, and pursue it. That very afternoon, Graham Cooke, a well-known conference speaker, came to Bethel and spoke on our *persona,* our identity in Heaven. He recommended that we take all of our prophetic words in which God speaks who we are in His eyes and believe and declare them. I felt that there was something happening in me and to me, and that God was even using a teacher to describe it to me.

I went to the Lord in prayer and asked what it was He wanted me to broker. He gave me a choice, but I suddenly felt a Divine download of five things, so I chose them all! Here are the Resources of Heaven I desire to broker:

1.) The *Father* **Heart of God** made available to all, that all may know their restored places as beloved sons and daughters — no orphans.

2.) **Full Salvation, Healing, and Deliverance** as provided through the finished work of the *Son,* Jesus Christ, in His death and resurrection.

3.) The exhilarating **Manifest Presence of God** in and

among us as experienced through the outpouring of His *Holy Spirit*.

4.) **Full and Abundant Provision** for Life and Godliness and for every good work, with all our needs supplied generously, according to His Plans, Purposes, and Promises from the beginning of creation, according to His Riches in Glory.

5.) The **Complete Authority** of the King, the Lord Jesus Christ, over all realms: physical, of the soul or unseen, and spiritual or supernatural — as delegated to His Kingdom Agents here on earth for the expansion of the dominion of His Kingdom into all the realms in this earth.

Then we had a meeting for our team that would be going to the Philippines in a few weeks. I met a young woman for the first time who would be on my team of four going to the Island of Mindanao. As we prophesied over each other, she drew a picture of me sinking into the quicksand of the Glory of God and coming out in a bubble-like room filled with gold for provision, spare body parts for healing, and a river signifying the refreshing and empowering Presence of God. I'd never told her anything about my new *persona*.

I believed that God was leading me into something new in my life, and I had been pursuing it and He had been meeting me. People's bills were actually getting paid, though I never knew how. That was fine with me, but I had one issue. I had really received $10,000 in Heaven, and I wanted to know what had become of it. The very next day He answered me.

I got a phone call from my son Jesse in Colorado. He was holding a letter that had been sent to my old address in Telluride and had then been forwarded to his post office box, as we had moved out of the area. He'd opened it to see if it was important and was now holding a check made out to me for $10,000. I laughed. When I asked God about it, I wanted to know if this was the money from Heaven, and was I supposed to use it to pay students' fees, or was it for Linda and me, as we could definitely use it. He told me I could do whatever I wanted with it, it was mine, and there was no best choice. Either way I chose to use it was good. Linda and I talked about it, and we felt that if we used it to Broker Heaven then it would open up more opportunities, and we could grow in the ever-increasing experience. We both only regretted that I hadn't thought to ask for more on my initial visit to the Treasury. We could easily have made a larger plan for the distribution of it. But I began to realize that since I had been there once and the abundance of it was limitless, I had continued future access to it.

It was immense fun to find students who had needs and to anonymously pay their school fees. I actually had so much fun that I ended up overpaying. I needed to get it all done before I left for the Philippines, so in my haste I had given away too much. But I made a trip back to the Treasury Room with a new plan and a new figure, and I'm waiting to see how this one pans out. I also put in a bid for a long list of healing miracles, as they are part of the resources of Heaven that I get to broker. Most of them came through on the epic trip to the Philippines that month, where we witnessed healings in unprecedented numbers. *Thank You, Lord. You are Good. Now, about the rest of that money....*

AFTERWORD

We've just taken a whirlwind tour through 38 years of adventures. The times spent in Colorado, Russia, Africa, the Philippines, Europe, California, and the Rainbow Gatherings contain enough miracles that books could be written about each of them. Perhaps those books are for another day. What's on my mind as I close this writing is to ask any of you who have been a part of any of the stories contained in this book to give me feedback. Do you remember other details I've forgotten? Do you remember them differently? Have I missed something important? Have I handled a situation wrongly? It would be tragic, I feel, if you had such thoughts and didn't share them with me. So I welcome your input.

One other thing I've been asked on many occasions is, "What ever happened to Faith, your daughter?" Now there's a story. Our search for healing for her vision brought us into a deeper experience of God's love and His Presence in our lives, but also into many experiences of His complex and wonderful ways. Two prophetic words we received in the early years were crucial parts in the journey of her healing.

The first was a scene that a woman saw in the Spirit one day as she prayed for Faith. She saw Faith as a little girl standing in a pool of water, overshadowed by two tall trees. When Faith looked down at the water, it was crystal clear and beautiful, but the trees above her were bare and dark, like the cold, dead trees of winter. Then when she looked up, the trees were full of leaves and glorious blossoms, filling the sky above her with fragrance and beauty. But the water under her was now a muddy pool that she did not see. We understood from this that what Faith saw might be different from what others could see, and that she might see things that we didn't.

Another woman prayed for Faith and then prophesied that when she was 17 years old she would seek God herself for her healing. This was less encouraging, as we were expecting a complete healing well before she reached that age. We actually forgot that prophecy and didn't think of it again for many years.

The doctors told us that Faith was born with cataracts that fully covered both eyes. We had prayed faithfully for two and a half years for her eyesight to become perfect, and we struggled with the idea of submitting her to a surgery that would remove the lenses from her eyes. We consented in the summer of 1979 when Faith was two and a half and went to Denver Children's Hospital for the operation. In the midst of the pale, sickly children in that place, she was a sun-browned bundle of health and energy. Many of the stories we encountered there broke our hearts.

Faith was in surgery for hours, and we spent a lot of the time in the hospital chapel praying. At one point I saw in the Spirit a mighty flood of glory and light come into the hospital at the ground floor. As the waters of light and thick glory rose up in the building from floor to floor, I saw hordes of dark, bat-like demons of sickness and disease being forced out of the building, leaping through windows and off the roof. I sensed the entire hospital was being filled with the healing power of Jesus.

We had hoped the operation would result in some

sort of improvement in Faith's vision, but when we met with the doctor he was extremely discouraging. He told us that she would never really see any better and that her retinas were undeveloped, so that she would never be able to distinguish color. The best they had done was to allow more light in, but she now had no lenses with which to focus that light. We were extremely frustrated, after having been pressured by numerous medical professionals to go ahead with this serious operation that this doctor now told us had been virtually ineffective. I had to work to maintain peace.

Faith's first post-op visit to the doctor proved to be an initial fulfillment of the prophecy of the trees. As she walked into the examination room, she dropped her bag of almonds, which spilled all over the floor. The linoleum floor was a tan color and had brown spots all over it, about the size and shape of raw almonds. The doctor watched in wonder as Faith went to each almond to pick it up and place it back in her bag, never reaching out to touch the spots, never mistaking the two. "She can't do that!" he exclaimed. And when she sat in the chair for him to inspect her eyes, she noticed a calendar on his wall across the room that was like the one I had at home. "Hey, Dad, that's the same picture you have on your wall." "She can't see that. That's impossible!" was his response.

And so began our adventure of never really knowing or understanding just what Faith could see. Color was all-important to her; she defined people by the colors they wore. She learned to read; she learned to read music and to play the piano as well as participating in the high school band. At 17 she fulfilled the prophecy, which we had since forgotten, by asking her friends to pray with her; she was ready to be healed and went after it! She went to college and has traveled the world. One time she flew by herself from the U.S. to England, changed *airports*, not just planes, and flew to South Africa for the winter to work as a nanny, then to Russia to stay with friends of ours for a month. She has a strong, independent streak and a determination to do anything she sets her mind and heart to. She also has the faith to believe God for the finances to do it.

The one thing that bothered her most was not being able to drive. Because she was declared legally blind she could not get her driver's license, and it frustrated her to be dependent on others to get around.

It became her goal to drive. A friend began to teach her in his truck on back roads, and then on the highway. We decided to give it another shot and went to an eye doctor in Grand Junction. He amazed us with the report that her eyesight was "not that bad." He thought it may have improved. Then he told us that there are lots of drivers on the road whose vision is worse than hers. Though that freaked us out a bit, it delighted her. She passed her driving test, bought a new car, and has put over 45,000 miles on it in two years! She is now a businesswoman, running a bed and breakfast in a mountain resort town in Colorado and working with the Chamber of Commerce to coordinate events in the area. I still don't know *how* she sees, but it's working out well for her. *You're amazing, God. Keep it up!*

Made in the USA
San Bernardino, CA
23 June 2018